Kuntao Jiu-Jitsu: Immediate Survival
A Realistic Self-Defense "Crash Course"
For Men and Women

Kuntao Jiu-Jitsu
Immediate Survival

A Realistic Self-Defense "Crash Course"
For Men and Women
Marc Bochner

Marc Bochner

Order this book online at www.trafford.com/07-2259
or email orders@trafford.com

Most Trafford titles are also available at major online book retailers.

© Copyright 2008 Marc Bochner.
Edited by Eli Glatt and Kendra Durney.
Cover design/Artwork by Lara Faustino.
Photography by Morris Bochner.
All rights reserved. No part of this publication may be reproduced, stored in a retrieval system, or transmitted, in any form or by any means, electronic, mechanical, photocopying, recording, or otherwise, without the written prior permission of the author.

Note for Librarians: A cataloguing record for this book is available from Library and Archives Canada at www.collectionscanada.ca/amicus/index-e.html

Printed in Victoria, BC, Canada.

ISBN: 978-1-4251-5165-2

We at Trafford believe that it is the responsibility of us all, as both individuals and corporations, to make choices that are environmentally and socially sound. You, in turn, are supporting this responsible conduct each time you purchase a Trafford book, or make use of our publishing services. To find out how you are helping, please visit www.trafford.com/responsiblepublishing.html

Our mission is to efficiently provide the world's finest, most comprehensive book publishing service, enabling every author to experience success. To find out how to publish your book, your way, and have it available worldwide, visit us online at www.trafford.com/10510

www.trafford.com

North America & international
toll-free: 1 888 232 4444 (USA & Canada)
phone: 250 383 6864 ♦ fax: 250 383 6804
email: info@trafford.com

The United Kingdom & Europe
phone: +44 (0)1865 722 113 ♦ local rate: 0845 230 9601
facsimile: +44 (0)1865 722 868 ♦ email: info.uk@trafford.com

10 9 8 7 6 5 4 3 2

DISCLAIMER

READ BEFORE PROCEEDING WITH ANY TRAINING

The techniques, weapons, drills, and other information contained/described herein are intended for personal and/or professional legitimate self-defense in accordance with all applicable laws and regulations in your city, state, and country, and are not to be used with any illegal intentions.

In any martial art, there is an assumption of risk. Please use caution.

Misuse, excessive force and/or misinterpretation of the concepts described/contained herein is at the reader's own risk, and could result in legal action, injury, or death. The purchase and study of this book does not equate to certification to teach Kuntao Jiu-Jitsu.

Nothing herein is implied.

The author(s), contributor(s), and/or publisher(s) of this book are not responsible in any manner whatsoever for any injury(ies) sustained from practice and/or following of instructions given within.

It is essential to consult with your physician and/or professional trainer before beginning the study of Kuntao Jiu-Jitsu, since the activities described herein may be too strenuous in nature for some readers to engage in safely.

All Rights Reserved.

No part of this publication may be reproduced or utilized in any form or by any means, electronic or mechanical, including photocopying, recording, or by any information storage and/or retrieval system, without written permission from the author, Marc Bochner.

Statements from the *Gift of Fear* and *Protecting the Gift: Keeping Children and Teenagers Safe (and Parents Sane)* have been clearly marked and are copyrighted by Gavin de Becker

Turning this page indicates that you have read, understood, and accepted the above statements.

Acknowledgements

I would like to thank the following people for assisting me in finishing this manual. Professor Bruce DiTraglia, Sensei Matthew Mendillo, Sensei Brian Baccaire, Eli Glatt, Kendra Durney, Sean Murphy, Morris Bochner, Gail Bochner, Ron Chatell, Dan Chatell, Kevin Leddy, Erin Cairney, Shannon McClure, Larry Minick, Patrick Saul, Jerri Cantone, Tessa Iannelli, Ron Malo, Lara Faustino, Makoto Osaki, and Chris Medeiros.

Dedication

To Celia, Samuel, Evelyn, Cagney and Pluto

To all the readers who are taking a stand in learning
how to defend themselves, their family, or their friends.

Foreword

I would like to thank you for taking the time to purchase and read this book on *Kuntao Jiu-Jitsu: Immediate Survival*. My intention for writing this book was to provide an average person, one who cannot commit to the extensive study of Kuntao Jiu-Jitsu, the necessary skills to survive a life-threatening situation.

The Crash Course, due to its effective techniques and easiness to comprehend, consists of the curriculum that is taught at on-site corporate seminars, self-defense workshops, and rape prevention seminars.

As with the adult and children official training manuals, if you are reading this book in addition to taking instruction at an official Kuntao Jiu-Jitsu dojo, I would suggest using the book as a guideline, highlighting the important concepts and making personal notes.

If you have purchased this book independently from training with an official Kuntao Jiu-Jitsu instructor, I would recommend to read each chapter carefully and to take diligent notes of the concepts and techniques. If a situation arises where you are confused about a topic or conceptual understanding, feel free to log on to the website www.KuntaoJiuJitsu.com and email me.

To help facilitate your learning of the concepts and techniques I have decided to include "particles of information" throughout the book. These particles can be used as a quick reference guide when trying to understand the information and are depicted with a ※. The particles can range from vital information about the current technique to references from previous chapters. Some of the particles also contain additional information that will benefit you throughout your training.

To get the most out of this manual, you need to develop the correct mindset: one of survival at all costs. To help you develop this, I have taken an excerpt out of Robert Greene's *The 33 Strategies of War*, which on page 124 he talks about human nature: "First, people are more likely to attack you if they see you as weak or vulnerable. Second, they cannot know for sure that you're weak; they depend of the signs you give out, through your behavior both present and past. Third, they are after easy victories, quick and bloodless. That is why [people] prey on the vulnerable and weak."

If you are having trouble retaining the information, remember the key to learning is to make the information your own. Learn from this book, apply it to your training, and keep the information that is relevant to your needs. If you would like to learn more about Kuntao Jiu-Jitsu please visit www.KuntaoJiuJitsu.com. There you may purchase the official training manual; *Kuntao Jiu-Jitsu: Your Guide to Realistic Self-Defense and Street Survival* and the official instructional six DVD box set.

Sincerely,
Soke-Dai Marc Bochner

Table of Contents

Chapter One: What is Kuntao Jiu-Jitsu? 1

Chapter Two: What is The Crash Course In Self-Defense? 2

Chapter Three: How to Not Be a Victim 3

Chapter Four: Conviction of Survival 6

Chapter Five: Managing Your Fear 7

Chapter Six: Intuition and Survival Instincts 9

Chapter Seven: Have a Game Plan 11

Chapter Eight: Weaknesses of the Human Body 12

Chapter Nine: Verbal Defusing 15

Chapter Ten: Self-Defense Stances 16

Chapter Eleven: Hand and Leg Striking Techniques 19

Chapter Twelve: Striking Combinations 35

Chapter Thirteen: Defending Against a Striking Adversary 41

Chapter Fourteen: Choking Techniques 58

Chapter Fifteen: Choke and Grab Defenses 60

Chapter Sixteen: Rape Prevention 138

Chapter Seventeen: Using Your Keys 145

Chapter Eighteen: If You Get Pushed To The Ground 148

Chapter Ninteen: Be Offensive On The Ground 157

Chapter Twenty: Closing Comments 168

About The Author 169

Founder of Kuntao Jiu-Jitsu 172

Kuntao Jiu-Jitsu Instructors 174

A Realistic Self-Defense "Crash Course"

Chapter One: What is Kuntao Jiu-Jitsu?

Kuntao Jiu-Jitsu is a hybrid martial art system that was formed by combining different aspects of martial art styles into one highly effective form of self-defense. Soke Richard Petronelli, the founder of Kuntao Jiu-Jitsu, has spent over forty years of his life dedicated to the conceptual understanding of various martial arts such as Kuntao, an Indonesian martial art specializing in low level strikes, Jiu Jitsu, Judo, Arnis, Tuite or nerve striking, Aikido, and Kung Fu. Kuntao Jiu-Jitsu incorporates an extensive ground fighting curriculum as well as elements from the art of Muay Thai Kickboxing. To round out the Kuntao Jiu-Jitsu system, fear management, verbal defusing techniques, and mindset training are also incorporated.

Why Does Kuntao Jiu-Jitsu Include More Than One Art?

Kuntao Jiu-Jitsu was formed because one martial arts style could not cover all concepts of realistic self-defense. Soke Petronelli followed in the footsteps of his instructor Professor Florendo Visitacion and created a hybrid system that is designed to give children and adults realistic self-defense knowledge. Living in today's society, a person needs to understand the many elements of self-defense, including:

Mental Aspects
- Understanding of Realistic Self-Defense Concepts
- How to Manage Fear
- How to Utilize Survival Instincts
- Learning to Trust Your Intuition
- The Anatomy of the Human Body
- Biomechanics of the Human Body

Physical Aspects
- How to Block and/or Evade an Adversary's Attack
- How to Use Effective Hand and Elbow Strikes
- How to Use Effective Leg and Knee Strikes
- How to Be Effective in the Four Ranges of Combat
- How to Be Effective Against Trained Adversaries
- Knowledge of Ukemi – Rolling/Falling
- Judo Throwing
- Jiu Jitsu Joint Manipulations
- Defenses from Grabbing Techniques
- How to Defend Yourself While on the Ground
- How to Defend Against Weapons (Stick/Gun/Knife)

Chapter Two: What is The Crash Course In Self-Defense?

What is the Crash Course?

The Kuntao Jiu-Jitsu Crash Course is the system of Kuntao Jiu-Jitsu stripped down to its core. Only the most vital and important concepts and techniques taught in Kuntao Jiu-Jitsu were extracted. The course teaches you how to perform basic hand, elbow, leg, and knee strikes, and how to use them effectively against an adversary. This manual effectively shows you how to defend yourself from over 40 scenarios including: an adversary trying to strike you, an adversary who is trying to choke you, defenses from inside a car, as well as defenses while sitting at a table. In addition, two Bonus Chapters will focus on ground survival, teaching you how to fall to the ground without getting injured, as well as applying Jiu-Jitsu joint manipulations from the ground.

What is the Intention of the Kuntao Jiu-Jitsu Crash Course?

- The Crash Course provides an effective self-defense course for all people who wish to learn self-defense in a short period of time.
- The program teaches basic skills that a person would need to survive in a life-threatening altercation.
- The course works highly off intuition and basic survival mechanisms that are already ingrained in your mind and body.
- To round out the course, full body suits are worn by instructors, so students can actually see and feel what it is like to apply forceful strikes to an attacker.
- While the program is not a cure-all self-defense course, it is the solid foundation of our method of realistic self-defense.

Remember:

All techniques need to be practiced on a regular basis in and out of class to achieve the most effective results.

What can you do after the completion of the Crash Course?

As with many of our students, if you are still interested in our method of realistic self-defense, you might enjoy the entire art of Kuntao Jiu-Jitsu. If you would like to learn more about Kuntao Jiu-Jitsu please visit www.KuntaoJiuJitsu.com. There you may purchase the official training manual; *Kuntao Jiu-Jitsu: Your Guide to Realistic Self-Defense and Street Survival* and the official instructional six DVD box set.

A Realistic Self-Defense "Crash Course"

Chapter Three: How to Not Be a Victim

The key to not becoming a victim is to understand how criminals/rapists pick their victims. A criminal (rapist) will choose **the easiest victim, one who is shy, unaware of his/her surroundings, and poses no threat to the attacker.** In this chapter, you should learn and memorize key strategies to avoid becoming a victim.

Safety Tip Number One: Be Aware

One of the most important strategies in remaining safe is to be aware and attentive to your surroundings. Make a mental image of everything around you. Make sure to remember key landmarks in case you get lost. Also, listen to your gut feeling (intuition) about the people around you. If an attacker notices that you are aware of your surroundings, he/she will no longer label you an easy target.

Safety Tip Number Two: Acknowledge Strangers

Assailants attack the weak and timid, not the bold and strong. (A bolder and stronger willed man or woman is more prone to fighting back against an assailant – something an adversary will not want.) If you are approached by a would-be-attacker, it is not ok for you to put your head down and keep walking. Instead, look directly at your assailant! This shows confidence as well as the ability to identify this person later on. This also shows your attacker that you acknowledge his/her presence, eliminating the element of surprise.

In the event that an adversary verbally approaches you walk away while keeping an eye on the stranger. Remember to have a pre-determined self-defense game plan, such as a hammer-fist, ready to strike in case the adversary does attack (Chapter 7).

Safety Tip Number Three: Hold Your Keys

Utilizing this tip, in addition to being aware of your surroundings, will help to prevent the majority of unwarranted attacks. Holding your keys in your hand with your largest key sticking out (more information Chapter 17), is an effective way to deter an adversary from attacking. Remember an attacker or rapist, wants the easiest target and before every attack they will scan their potential victim. If a potential victim is fully aware of his/her surroundings and is holding their keys in an offensive manner, the adversary may pass on choosing that person.

Safety Tip Number Four: Do Not Go Out Alone

Remember the aged old saying: use the buddy system and never go anywhere alone? Try to make daily concessions in your life, whether it be to ask a co-worker, whom you trust, to walk you to your car, or call a friend to accompany you to the local mall, keep safety in mind, and try to limit the time you go out alone. Corresponding to what we already know, attackers want the easiest victim; it will be very hard for an attacker to handle one, let alone two unwilling participants. Just like the previous step, following this rule, can potentially prevent an adversary from choosing you. You should also let a friend or relative know when you are going out and when you plan on returning.

Safety Tip Number Five: Have a Defensive Plan Ready (Chapter 7)
On the physical side of staying safe from strangers is the pre-determined self-defense game plan should you ever get attacked. We will go into more detail in the following chapters, but for now, understand that knowing how you are going to defend yourself before getting attacked is a vital key in effectively defending yourself. The most common pre-determined self-defense would be a simple strike, such as a hammer-fist to the face or groin or even a finger poke to the eyes.

Safety Tip Number Six: Fight Back
In the event that an assailant does approach you and either intimidates you verbally (with words) or physically (by placing his/her hands on you), you have the right to defend yourself. Remember attackers only want an easy person who cooperates. Using your Kuntao Jiu-Jitsu training such as a hammer-fist to the face, an open palm to the face, or front kick to the groin, will stop the majority of assailants from hurting you.

In addition to the physical act of fighting back, you should also understand that verbally telling your assailant "Stop Right Now" or "Do Not Touch Me" is a sign of assertiveness (a sign assailants will understand as "not this person").

In a ground altercation, striking your adversary in the face with your hammer-fist is a recommended technique.

A Realistic Self-Defense "Crash Course"

Staying Safe Check List

Staying Safe Tip #1
Be Aware of Your Surroundings.

Staying Safe Tip #2
Look Directly at a Stranger Who Comes Up To You (Make Eye Contact).

Staying Safe Tip #3
Be Assertive, Bold, and Confident.

Staying Safe Tip #4
Try To Limit The Times You Go Out Alone.

Staying Safe Tip #5
Never Go With an Attacker.

Staying Safe Tip #6
Always Look In Your Backseat Before Entering Your Vehicle.

Staying Safe Tip #7
Do Not Walk Between Parked Cars, As Someone Could Be Waiting For You.

Staying Safe Tip #8
Know It Is Ok To Fight Back.

Staying Safe Tip #9
Practice Predetermined Self-Defense and Have Your Hammer-fist Ready To Strike.

Staying Safe Tip #10
Remember Being Safe Is More Important Than Being Polite To a Stranger.

Particle of Information: Appearance of an Adversary
A potential adversary is not some dark, frightening figure. He/she is an average person who looks exactly like you.

Chapter Four: Conviction of Survival

Before we get to the physical part of this manual, we need to cover the reason why **you will survive in any altercation**. This main psychological factor of survival is your conviction or will to survive. This conviction will overcome all the fears and emotions that precede a potentially violent situation. It is normal to have doubts about your self-defense abilities, especially if you have never before been forced to defend yourself. This conviction is an internal feeling where nothing, not even your self-doubt or an adversary, will stand in the way of your survival. Your only focus should be on surviving and getting back to your loved ones.

Although developing the conviction will be different for every reader there are key factors in helping to unlock your will to survive:

- You must have a powerful emotion or memory that invokes a sense of determination.
- You must have the mindset that this or any adversary is not going to be responsible for ruining or changing your life.
- You must have confidence in yourself.

Once you get the feeling, that powerful emotion, that you that you control your life, you must hone your new skill. Use this emotional advantage in your training, when you are practicing your basic strikes and self defense techniques and if you are ever involved in a life-threatening altercation. Remember just like your physical skills, your conviction must be practiced until it is ingrained into your mind.

Concept Reminder:

Your Will To Survive Will Triumph Any Adversary's Desire To Harm You

A Realistic Self-Defense "Crash Course"

Chapter Five: Managing Your Fear

The following chapter deals with the emotion of fear – how to identify it, how to deal with it, and eventually how to control it. Learning to overcome your fear is a valuable tool in arriving at the right mindset to defend yourself. In a life-threatening situation, you should be confident in your skills and believe that you will survive. No one is going to stand in the way of you getting back to your loved ones.[1]

Understand Your Fear

When faced with a situation in which you feel threatened, the overwhelming fear of getting hurt, injured, or humiliated is enough to paralyze even the most dedicated martial artists. Fear is a powerful emotion that can have a crippling effect. In Gavin de Becker's book *The Gift Of Fear,* he writes "True fear is a survival signal that sounds only in the presence of danger, yet unwarranted fear has assumed a power over us that it holds over no other creature on earth" (de Becker 1997 333). De Becker also states that "Real fear is a signal intended to be very brief, a mere servant of intuition" (336).

When you have "stage fright," a symptom of fear, you become momentarily paralyzed. In a life-threatening situation, standing still is severely debilitating and yields very poor and harmful results. Simply stated, uncontrolled fear stops you from defending yourself. If you do not train yourself to acknowledge fear, you are doing yourself a great injustice. In de Becker's book, he states the first rule of fear: "The very fact that you fear something is solid evidence that it is not happening" (341).

How to Mentally Deal With Fear

The key to controlling your fear is developing the proper mindset. While each student will develop his/her own way of mentally preparing to deal with fear, one of the first concepts you must learn is that fear warns you that something *might* happen. If it does happen, we stop fearing it and start to respond to it, manage it, or surrender to it. De Becker also reminds us that fear can be perceived as good news, because it confirms that the dreaded outcome has not yet (if it even will) occurred.

You must understand that when you get into a life-threatening situation, fear will be right there with you. Knowing that fear is going to accompany you in times of need is a brave step in the proper direction to controlling your fear. De Becker states that "When you accept the survival signal as a welcome message and quickly evaluate the environment or situation, fear stops in an instant. Trusting intuition is the exact opposite of living in fear" (336).

---

[1] Chapters 5 and 6 were both supplemented by Gavin de Becker's book *The Gift of Fear*. See reference page.

How Your Body Deals With Fear

The human body is designed with intense emotions (such as fear) as feedback systems. If humans did not possess fear, they would not be able to identify life-threatening situations because there would be no emotional response to the fear-inducing stimuli. While fear gives us the advantage of avoiding perilous situations, it also has the disadvantage of preventing us from doing what has to be done - in this case defending ourselves. Fortunately, when we sense fear, our body reacts by producing mass amounts of adrenaline. Released from the adrenal glands located at the apex of the kidneys, this adrenaline can be compared to a surge of immense energy that can and should be used to defend yourself.

Effects of Adrenaline

Adrenaline has many positive effects on the body that are characterized by periods of immense strength, an increase in speed, and an increased tolerance to pain. On the downside, fear also creates a decrease in fine motor skills. This means that techniques that are too complex to execute will fail miserably in stressful situations. This is the main reason why it is more important to be able to flow and create effective techniques rather then try to pull off a precise move learned in the dojo.

Positive Effects:
1. Increased strength
2. Increased speed
3. Increased tolerance to pain

Negative Effects:
1. Decreased fine motor skills

In the event where an adversary attacks you from behind, your adrenaline can be used to facilitate your defense.

Chapter Six: Intuition and Survival Instincts

In this chapter, we will cover two paramount traits that will save your life, regardless of skill level. These two life-preserving internal mechanisms, human intuition and basic instincts, will be hard at work prior to, during, and after a life-threatening altercation.

To facilitate this concept, review the following scenario:

Maria, a young businesswoman, has been working late to finish up a financial project at work. Being a very attentive young woman, she notices that the sky is pitch black and understands that it would not be wise to walk to her car alone. Since there are no fellow employees around, she phones security to see if someone can escort her to her vehicle. After several attempts to contact security, she ultimately decides to brave it alone.

As she leaves the office building the empty parking lot becomes quite clear. She heads off to her car that she can vaguely see in the distance. Maria makes it halfway to her car before she sees a man in the distance. With no one else in sight and keys in hand, Maria continues to walk towards her car. As she continues, she notices the man moving faster. Something (intuition) in Maria's head told her that this was the time to make her stand, so she stopped by one of the lighted areas of the parking lot next to an emergency phone. By this time the man was in close proximity. Facing the man, eyes attentive, standing straight up, and with a large key in hand, Maria asserts herself and asked the man "Is there a reason why you are following me?" Without a sound the man walked by Maria, all the while Maria's eyes stayed attentive ready to defend herself with a forceful strike of her key. Maria then watched as the man made a surprising turn about and headed back to where he came. When he was no longer in sight,

Maria, remaining attentive, headed to her car and like all alert individuals she checked the backseat before she got in. As she got in her vehicle, she immediately locked her doors and drove home safely.

In *The Gift of Fear*, de Becker states that "intuition is a cognitive process, faster than we recognize and far different from the familiar step-by-step thinking we rely on so willingly" (de Becker 1997 28). He goes on to state that "we predict the behavior of other human beings based on our ability to read certain signals that we recognize" (108). In the aforementioned scenario, Maria knew it was not smart to go to her car alone. However when she "sensed" she was being followed she allowed her instincts to take over.

The answers to all of these questions were in her, just like they are inside you and me. As de Becker points out "instead of being grateful to have a powerful internal resource, grateful for the self-care, instead of entertaining the possibility that our minds might actually be working for us and not just playing tricks on us, we rush to ridicule the impulse. We, in contrast to every other creature in nature, choose not to explore and even to ignore – survival signals. The mental energy we use searching for the innocent explanation to everything could more constructively be applied to evaluating the environment for important information" (34).

Showing that you are assertive may cause your attacker to flee. Unlike the logical thinking that you are used to, de Becker states that intuition:

1) Is always in response to something.
2) Always has your best interest at heart (de Becker 1997 82).

He warns that "judgment, an added ingredient in human nature, gives us the ability to disregard our instincts until you can explain it logically" (33). Unfortunately, many victims have fallen prey to this unwarranted survival procedure.

Why Rely On Your Survival (Basic) Instincts?

- Basic instincts are executed quickly, while choreographed moves tend to take longer to execute.
- Traditional dojo techniques are often too complicated and intricate to perform under stressful situations.
- Nothing will go as planned. Sticking to one technique or movement without adapting to your situation can result in major injuries.

How Does Kuntao Jiu-Jitsu Increase Your Chances for Survival?

The art of Kuntao Jiu-Jitsu relies highly on the ability of adaptation. We, the instructors, understand that not everything, and maybe nothing, will go as planned. Just as with your intuition, you cannot logically map out your next defensive measure step-by-step when engaged in a violent altercation. When an adversary is punching you, you must be able to react instinctively. If one move is rendered ineffective, you must have additional options that you are ready to immediately employ. Without this conceptual understanding, many martial artists will try to use set defensive techniques that will fail miserably in a violent altercation. Imagine spending years perfecting a bear hug defense and when you utilize it, the adversary reacts in a different manner than how you thought he/she would.

Remember that "nature's greatest accomplishment, the human brain, is never more efficient or invested than when its host is at risk" (de Becker 1997 28).

Particle of Information: Intuition

Trust your instincts. Many victims of violent assaults reported that before they were physically attacked, they had an inclination that something bad was going to happen. Listen to your instincts and you might just avoid a life-threatening situation.

Chapter Seven: Have a Game Plan

One of the most effective and practical self-defense concepts in realistic self-defense is to have a game plan. Know what you are going to do and how you are going to strike your adversary before anything happens! (Also known as Predetermined Self-Defense) Predetermined self-defense means that you know how you are going to defend yourself before the adversary attempts to attack you. Predetermined self-defense allows you to choose in advance one strike or a combination of strikes, thus eliminating any confusion as to how you are going to initially defend yourself. Using predetermined self-defense allows for a quick defense that is more effective than choosing your defense based on how your adversary attacks you (because by that time, you have already been attacked). As you are reading this manual, I would suggest to learn the basic strikes and come up with two different predetermined self-defense game plans that you would be able to use in a potential situation. Remember practice predetermined self-defense diligently because the faster you strike your adversary, the quicker you go home.

Why Have a Game Plan?
1. Having a game plan allows quicker execution of a move or strike.
2. Knowing what you are going to do before a physical attack occurs may reduce your fear.
3. The first physical strike is often the hardest. Having a game plan will allow you to execute it quickly and then enter into a survival mode.

Game Plan Examples:
1. Hammer-fist to your adversary's face.
2. Open Palm Strike to your adversary's face or groin.
3. Finger Poke to your adversary's eyes or throat.
4. Knee to your adversary's groin.

Remember, any game plan has to be diligently practiced in different situations. If an adversary walks up to you and you feel threatened you should elect to strike first. Show your attacker you are not a man or woman who is going to be taken advantaged of.

After Your Game Plan Is Executed
The first few strikes are all you can logically map out in a self-defense situation. After your game plan, you must then rely on your survival instincts and self-defense training. Remember, the paramount objective is to get away safely and back to your family and loved ones.

Chapter Eight: Weaknesses of the Human Body

    The human body is an amazing, fascinating, and complex mechanism. The way the body can move, adapt, and undergo change is essential for our survival. However, even with all the amazing things our body can do for us, it still maintains certain limitations and weak points. When weak areas of the body are properly struck, you can effectively stop an attack, and in some cases drop your adversary to the ground. Properly striking these regions of the body will also create enough time for you to run away and get help.

Caution:
Remember some strikes can cause serious injury or death if used with excessive force.

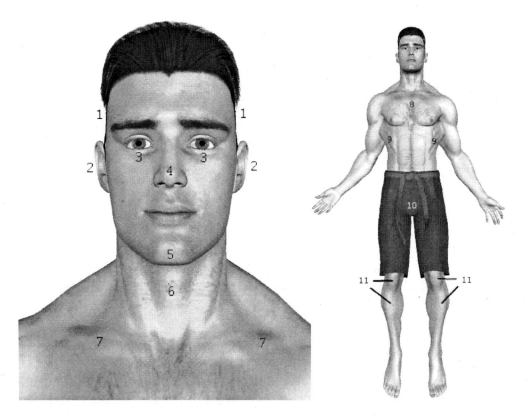

A Realistic Self-Defense "Crash Course"

Vital Areas of the Human Body

Vital Area #1: Temple
The temple regions, located on either side of the human head, can become a very sensitive area when struck. A direct strike to the temple could cause severe head trauma and possible death. The most effective way to affect the temple region is with a close-fisted strike.

Vital Area #2: Ears
The ears are a delicate part of the human body that can be properly affected in a couple of ways. The first way to affect your adversary's ears is to box them, using two open palms. Boxing the ears refers to striking the ears simultaneously in a quick and direct movement. If done correctly, this will disorientate your adversary, allowing you to run away to safety or, if you must, continue your defensive strategy. The ears can also be affected by using a downward pulling motion. Pulling your adversary's ear downward with enough force can possibly tear off the ear.

Vital Area #3: Eyes
A properly executed finger poke to the eyes will unbalance your adversary and make him/her instinctively cover his/her face. Striking this vital area will also cause your opponent's eyes to water and possibly cause temporary and/or permanent blindness.

The most effective way to affect the eyes is with a finger poke or a face rake. When striking the eyes with a finger poke, make sure you use all of your fingers.

Vital Area #4: Nose
A properly executed strike to the nose will cause the adversary's eyes to water and their nose to bleed. This results in severe pain and temporary blindness. The most effective way to affect the nose region is with a hammer fist, an open palm, or a close-fisted strike.

Vital Area #5: Chin
The chin is another vital area that can be affected in several different ways. The first way to affect the chin is a correctly executed strike to the Trigeminal nerve, which is located on the sides of the chin. A direct hit can render a person unconscious. The chin can also be affected by using an open palm strike in an upward motion. Using this strike will cause your adversary to fall backwards.

Vital Area #6: Throat
A properly executed strike to the throat region can be a very effective way to deter your adversary from continuing his/her attack. If struck correctly, it will cause your adversary to drop back and possiblly fall to the ground. Remember that gagging and possible death could occur if you strike this area with excessive force.

Kuntao Jiu-Jitsu: Immediate Survival

Vital Area #7: Collarbone

A devastating strike with extreme power directed at collarbone could cause it to fracture, and result in splintering. The splintering of the bone could lead to permanent injury or death. The collarbone is best affected with a downward strike such as a hammer-fist.

Vital Area #8: Breastbone

The breastbone is best affected with a punch directly to the center of your adversary's chest. A solid strike to the breastbone can cause it to fracture and possibly splinter inside your adversary.

Vital Area #9: Ribs

The ribs are designed to withstand a downward blow. Therefore, using an upward strike, placed under the ribs can impact the underlying nerves. This solid blow upward can fracture the ribs. Breaking your adversary's ribs will make it difficult for your attacker to expand his/her diaphragm, which will cause difficulty in breathing.

Vital Area #10: Groin

A very sensitive area, striking a man or woman in the groin area can cause severe, debilitating pain. With enough force striking an adversary in the groin can also cause unconsciousness. The best way to affect the groin region is with a direct strike such as a front kick or knee strike.

Vital Area #11: Knees or Shins

Attacking the knees and shins of your adversary is an effective way to stop your adversary from striking you. Solid blows to these lower limbs can cause dislodging of the knee and breaking or fracturing of the tibia and fibula bones in the shin. The best ways to affect the lower limbs are front ball kicks and knees strikes.

Chapter Nine: Verbal Defusing

While storing your predetermined self-defense game plan in your head, you should always try to verbally defuse a situation in which your adversary is verbally attacking you. (If an altercation has turned physical and your adversary grabs or strikes you, a physical response is warranted.) Although verbal defusing will be unique depending on the situation there are guidelines you can follow. Akin to the rest of the manual, verbal defusing must be diligently practiced with a partner. Different scenarios should be rehearsed with either a successful or unsuccessful verbal outcome. If the verbal defusing is unsuccessful, a physical defense is your only option.

While it is not always possible to effectively defuse each situation, here are some guidelines for properly defusing a pending dispute:

Guideline One: Non-Threatening and Nonviolent
If an adversary approaches you, immediately assume your non-threatening position. In the verbal exchange express that you are not looking to fight. If you are no longer a threat to your adversary it may help to calm him/her down.

Guideline Two: Find out What Your Adversary Wants
When you find out what is causing your adversary to become hostile, you can possibly give him/her something to compensate. If you have caused your adversary to spill his/her drink, buy a new one.

Guideline Three: Appeal to Your Adversary's Ego
Boosting an adversary's ego with compliments might sway his/her idea of fighting.

Guideline Four: Have an Assertive, Yet Non-Threatening, Tone of Voice
While verbally defusing a situation, your tone of voice should be clear and assertive. Showing a potential adversary that you are not afraid is a key to verbally defusing a situation. Keep in mind, however, that being overly assertive might only escalate the situation.

Chapter Ten: Self-Defense Stances

This chapter deals with the initial positions that you will use throughout your training. In an altercation these stances must be instinctive and natural. Diligently practice each stance and understand when to use each.

Non-Threatening Position

The non-threatening position is used to calm down your adversary by showing him/her that you have no intention of fighting and that you possess no hidden weapons. Using the non-threatening position will allow you to assertively show your attacker that you acknowledge his/her presence. While giving you some time to plan your predetermined self-defense, the non-threatening position might possibly give your adversary a false sense of confidence, giving you the element of surprise when you strike.

How to perform a non-threatening position:
1. Stand erect.
2. Hold your hands up with your palms facing outward towards the adversary.

Although I am trying to verbally defuse the situation, I am physically ready to defend myself.

A Realistic Self-Defense "Crash Course"

Non-Threatening Position

Advantages of the Non-Threatening Position:

1. **Ready to Defend** - Your hands are up and ready to defend yourself.

2. **Calming Effect** - The non-threatening position can possibly calm down your adversary. This is due to the fact that you no longer appear to be a threat to your adversary. This could cause:

   - *Your adversary to walk away* – During a male vs. male altercation, being macho could be the cause of the altercation. If you are in your non-threatening position, you appear as if you are backing down. Since it is not macho or tough to fight a man who has already "given up," your adversary may elect to walk away.
   - *A drop in your adversary's adrenaline* – since you are no longer a "threat" to your adversary's safety, his/her body can respond by producing less adrenaline, while it gives your body time to release more.
   - *Lowering of your adversary's guard* – this will cause your adversary to "toy" with you by pushing or using a telegraphed punch, instead of employing an effective strategy.

3. **Element of Surprise** – You no longer seem like a "threat," so when you take action to defend yourself, your adversary will be surprised. Your adversary will have to overcome this sense of shock in order to adequately mount his/her original attack.

4. **False Sense of Confidence** – Your adversary will feel more confident in him/herself after seeing you "surrender." This confidence, however, will quickly turn into self doubt when you start to defend yourself.

5. **Legal Action** – People who observed the altercation will remember you having your hands up and verbally pleading not to fight. In a case in which you had to physically defend yourself, this testimony could be beneficial in a court of law.

Self-Defense Striking Stance

This section of the chapter covers how to stand when striking an adversary. Understand that maintaining a proper stance is crucial in becoming an effective striker. If you are involved in an altercation, you must learn how to strike while maintaining proper balance. If your balance is compromised at any point, your striking capabilities will be hindered.

Correct Self-Defense Striking Stance
1. Stand up straight with your hands up, palms facing outward.
2. Extend one leg slightly forward while keeping the toes of your opposite leg even with the heel of your forward leg.
3. Your feet should be shoulder width apart with your toes pointing forward.

Why Is This Stance Correct?
1. You are able to deliver quick and powerful hand and leg strikes.
2. You are able to block an adversary's attack.
3. You are able to withstand low kicks.
4. You are able to prevent takedowns.
5. You are able to initiate takedowns.

A Realistic Self-Defense "Crash Course"

Chapter Eleven: Hand and Leg Striking Techniques

In this chapter you will learn all the basic hand, elbow, leg and knee strikes needed to help you to survive a life-threatening situation. The main objective in self-defense is to strike the other person, causing confusion and doubt in your attacker. In the complete Kuntao Jiu-Jitsu system and the Crash Course all the techniques are based off of using these strikes, to enter in close, control and then finish you attacker.

Hand Strikes: Hammer-fist

The hammer-fist is one of the safest and quickest ways to end an altercation. As opposed to striking with the bones and knuckles of your hand, the hammer-fist uses the boneless part of your hand to strike your adversary.

How to Perform a Hammer-fist:

1. Make a fist with your hand: with your thumb on top.
2. Use the side of your clenched fist.
3. Extend your arm from your elbow downward.
4. Punch directly to and through your target.

Where to Strike with a Hammer-fist:
- Nose
- Side of Chin
- Groin

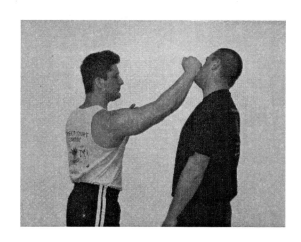

Caption Left: In this variation, I used my hammer-fist to strike the side of my adversary's chin. This will change his line of sight, making it easier for me to continue my defensive measures.

Hand Strikes: Open Palm

The open palm is a very direct and disorienting strike that can be used in several ways. The open palm can be used to thrust your adversary's chin upward or used to strike downward directly onto your adversary's nose. The open palm can also be used to "box" the ears, change the focus of your adversary, or drive the adversary backward.

How to Perform an Open Palm:

1. Open your hand so your palm faces your adversary.
2. Using your shoulder and elbow, extend your open palm directly into your adversary's nose or below the chin.
3. Drive your adversary backward.

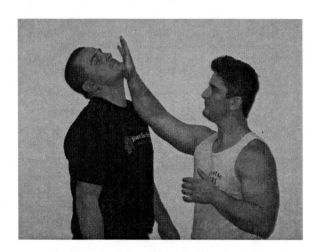

Where to Strike with an Open Palm:
- Ears
- Nose
- Chin
- Groin

Hand Strikes: Finger Poke

The finger poke is a strike that requires minimal power to execute and is designed to affect the eyes and throat of your adversary. When performing a finger poke, all of the fingers are extended outward as they drive into your target.

How to Perform a Finger Poke:

1. Extend all of your fingers outward.
2. Drive directly toward and through your target with your fingers pointed straight ahead.

Where to Strike with a Finger Poke:
- Eyes
- Throat

Hand Strikes: Face Rake

The face rake can best be described as making a claw-like formation with your hand. This "claw" is used to rake the face and the eyes of your adversary. For maximum effect, the face rake should be followed up by a more powerful strike such as a hammer-fist.

How to Perform a Face Rake:

1. Make a claw-like formation by flexing your fingers inward.
2. Using your fingers and nails, attack your target in a downward manner.

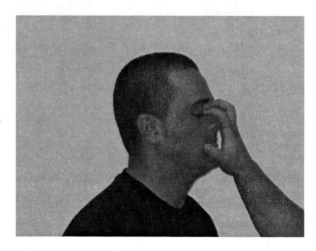

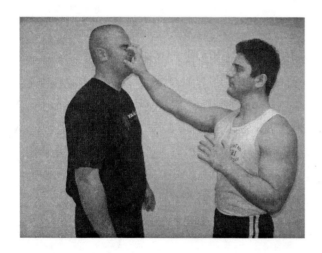

Where to Strike with a Face Rake:
- Face
- Eyes

A Realistic Self-Defense "Crash Course"

Hand Strikes: Elbow Strike

The elbow strike is a devastating strike that, like the open palm, can be used in a multitude of ways. It can be performed in a horizontal position, a vertical position, on a diagonal or as a back elbow. Due to the range deficit, the elbow strike is used only in a close-quarters position. When performing the strike from you self-defense striking stance, your back leg should be adjusted forward to increase the striking range.

How to Perform an Elbow Strike:

1. Start in your self-defense striking stance.
2. Bend your arm inward at your elbow.
3. In a horizontal motion use your elbow to strike the intended target.
4. To properly execute an elbow strike, use the rotation of your torso in conjunction with the rotation of your back foot.

Where to Strike with an Elbow:
- Head
- Chin
- Stomach
- Groin (Upward)
- Back
- Back of Neck (Lethal)

Caption Left: Notice when I deliver my elbow strike, my back leg will rotate on my toes. This allows full hip rotation and more power in my elbow strike.

Kuntao Jiu-Jitsu: Immediate Survival

Variation: Back Elbow

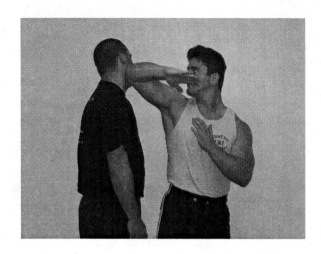

In this variation, I use my back elbow strike to strike my adversary's face.

In this variation, I use my back elbow strike to strike my adversary's stomach. From this point, I could also hammer-fist my adversary's groin.

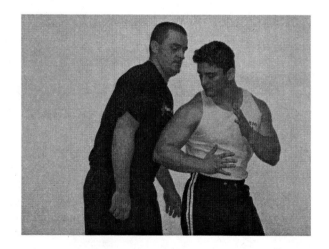

A Realistic Self-Defense "Crash Course"

Hand Strikes: Ridge Hand

Used in Judo takedowns such as an outer reap, the ridge hand uses the thumb side of your arm to strike your adversary. Tuck your thumb under your palm and use your wrist and forearm to strike the adversary in the chest, the throat, or the face.

How to Perform a Ridge Hand:

1. Horizontally flex your wrist outward, so that you are exposing your thumb side.
2. Tuck your thumb under your palm and use your wrist and your forearm to strike your target.
3. Keep your elbow bent and drive through your target.

Where to Strike with a Ridge Hand:
- Neck
- Groin

Caption Left: In this picture you can see my ridge hand striking my adversary's neck.

Kuntao Jiu-Jitsu: Immediate Survival

Hand Strikes: Box Ears

Boxing the ears of your adversary is a highly effective and quick way to end an altercation. Boxing the ears will immediately stun your adversary and corrupt the integrity of his/her balance. After you box your adversary's ears, it is advisable to either run away or use other strikes to end the altercation.

How to Box the Ears:

1. Raise your hands to the side of your adversary's face.
2. Use two open palms to simultaneously strike your adversary's ears.

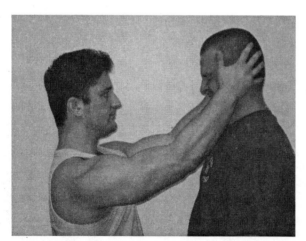

Where to Strike with an Ear Box:
- Ears

A Realistic Self-Defense "Crash Course"

Hand Strike: Closed Fisted Strike

Covering the final hand strike, we will want to review a close fisted strike. This strike, although highly effective, does need to be practiced to ensure that you do not sustain injury. The three key factors when using a closed fisted strike are to place your thumb on top of your fist and keep you hand positioned on a 45 degree angle so your ulna and radius bones are aligned. Finally, always strike your adversary with your first two knuckles.

How to Perform a Closed Fisted Strike:

1. Make a fist with your thumb placed on top.
2. Angle your fist on a 45 degree angle.
3. Strike your target with your first two knuckles.

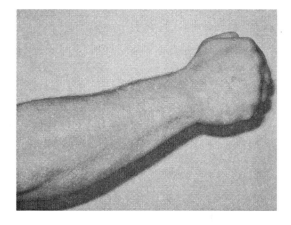

Where to Strike with a Closed Fist:
- Face
- Nose
- Chin
- Stomach
- Ribs
- Groin

Caption Left: When punching be certain to punch through your target.

Kicking Techniques

Leg Striking Techniques: Oblique Kick

The oblique kick is one of the more unique kicks in the art of Kuntao Jiu-Jitsu. The oblique kick is a quick and forceful strike that uses the bottom side of your foot to strike the adversary's shin, ankle or knee. A properly executed oblique kick can drop an adversary in seconds.

How to Perform an Oblique Kick:

1. Slide your foot off the ground and angle it so the ball of your foot is facing the adversary's shin and ankle.
2. Drive into the adversary's shin or ankle using the ball of your foot.

Where to Strike with an Oblique Kick:
- Shin
- Knee (45 Degree Angle)

Caption Left: Using my oblique kick on a 45 degree angle at my adversary's knee will cause it to buckle sending my adversary towards the floor. From this point, stomp your adversary's ankle.

Leg Striking Techniques: Front-ball Kick

A front-ball kick can be a very devastating kick when correctly executed. The front-ball kick is used most effectively to strike the nerves in the lower limbs of your adversary and it is also one of the more effective tools when fighting a boxer.

To Perform a Front-ball Kick:

1. Lift your knee upward.
2. Extend your leg forward using your knee as the fulcrum, or hinge.
3. Strike your adversary with the ball of your foot as you keep your toes pointed upward.
4. Drive through your target
5. After performing the kick, place the kicking leg close to your adversary. This will close the distance gap. Do not recoil your kicking leg.

Where to Strike with a Front Ball Kick:
- Groin
- Quadriceps
- Knee

Caption Left: Notice, when striking your adversary with a front ball kick to the lower extremity, it causes them to lean forward. From this position grab your adversary and deliver a knee to his/her stomach, groin, or head.

Leg Striking Techniques: Front Kick

The front kick is an effective way to strike your adversary's groin. To properly execute a front kick, lift your leg and extend it outward from your knee. The point of contact is made with the instep of your foot. A knee strike should be executed after a well placed front ball kick.

How to Perform a Front Kick:

1. Raise your knee upward.
2. Extend your leg outward from your knee, keeping your toes pointed downward.
3. Using the instep, or top of your foot, strike your adversary in the groin.

Where to Strike with a Front Kick:
- Groin

Leg Striking Techniques: Knee Strike

A knee strike is a very powerful strike that is performed from a clinched position. Your knees can effectively strike your adversary's head, body, or lower extremity. Due to the quickness of knee strikes, they are often used in combinations of three or four.

How to Perform a Knee Strike:

1. Clinch your adversary's head.
2. Lift and drive your knee into his/her face.

Where to Strike with a Knee Strike:
- Head
- Stomach
- Groin

Quick Strikes for Survival

Now that we have addressed the mechanics of the strikes utilized in Kuntao Jiu-Jitsu, it is beneficial to review eight highly effective strikes and the areas in which they are most devastating. During an altercation, it is a possibility that you may be become increasingly scared and "forget" your Kuntao Jiu-Jitsu training, these eight attacks can prove pivotal in your survival.

Starting Position
When an adversary approaches you, stand in a non-threatening position: hands open with your palms facing your adversary. If at all possible, try to verbally diffuse the situation, but be physically ready to strike. Do not clench your fists, as this will negate your verbal diffusing.

Open Palm to the Face
From your non-threatening position, thrust your open palm into your adversary's face. Aim for the chin or the nose, as this will cause your adversary's head to move backwards. If possible, immediately run to safety or continue your defense with a front kick to the groin.

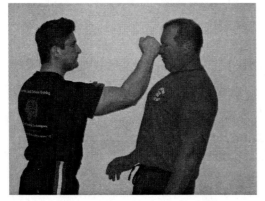

Hammer-fist to the Nose
From your non-threatening position, use the side of your clenched fist to strike your adversary's nose. In the scenario where your adversary leans forward, clinch his/her head and knee your adversary in the face. When your adversary is dazed, throw him/her to the ground and run to safety.

A Realistic Self-Defense "Crash Course"

Box the Ears
From your non-threatening position, use two open palms to simultaneously strike your adversary's ears. Hold onto your adversary's head and use a knee to strike the groin. With your adversary leaning forward, throw your adversary to the ground, stomp his/her ankle, and run to safety.

Box the Ears/Thumb Gouge the Eyes
As an alternative to the previous scenario, first box your adversary's ears. With your hands still on your adversary's head, use your thumbs to gouge into your adversary eyes. From this position, it will be beneficial to knee your adversary in the groin, throw the adversary to the ground, stomp the ankle, and run to safety.

Finger Poke/Face Rake the Eyes
While in your non-threatening position, use all of your fingers to strike into your adversary's eyes. From this position, flex your fingers into a "claw-like" configuration. Apply a downward force, raking your adversary's face. Run to safety.

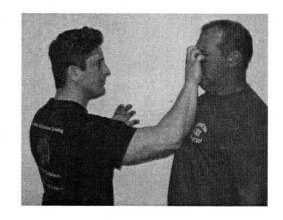

Kuntao Jiu-Jitsu: Immediate Survival

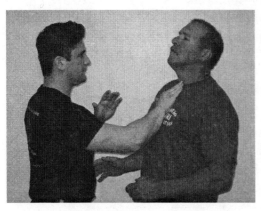

Finger Poke to the Throat
Use all of your fingers to strike into your adversary's throat. The stunning effect of this strike will allow you to follow up with either a hammer-fist or an open palm to the face.

Front Kick to the Groin
When your adversary is approaching you, you may choose to use a pre-determined self-defense such as a front kick to strike your adversary's groin. With your adversary leaning forward, either continue with knee strikes or run to safety.

Frontball Kick to the Inner Thigh or Knee
As an alternative to striking your adversary's groin, you may elect to perform a frontball kick to your adversary's knee, or inner thigh. Again with your adversary leaning forward, either continue with knee strikes or run to safety.

Keep in mind, these strikes can severely debilitate your adversary,

proceed with caution!

A Realistic Self-Defense "Crash Course"

Chapter Twelve: Striking Combinations

To successfully defend yourself, you must be able to use your strikes in effective combinations. The objective of striking in combinations is to stun you adversary and get in close, as quickly as possible. When practicing the combinations in the dojo there will be a few different methods in which to perform them. When performing the combinations on hand mitts, you are honing your speed and accuracy of your strikes. In contrast, when you are performing combinations on the heavy bags, you are working your power and endurance. To be a successful and effective striker, you must practice both methods.

Keep in mind that in a real altercation, after you have stunned your adversary with your strikes, you must clinch him/her and control his/her body.

Understand that fights are dynamic and they include motion. When you strike your adversary, it will result in additional motion within you and your adversary. If your strikes are causing your adversary to move away from you, it is imperative that you either run away or clinch to stop your adversary's momentum. Clinching will also hinder your attacker's ability to continue fighting. Clinching is a generalized term that means to grab hold of your adversary. Clinching can be accomplished with a Muay Thai clinch, or with a simple grabbing technique.

Muay Thai Front Clinch

In the Muay Thai front clinch, cup your hands together and place them behind your adversary's neck. From this position, pull your adversary's head in and down towards your body keeping your elbows tight. At this point, you can easily strike your adversary with your knee and elbow strikes.

Overhooks

As an alternative to the traditional clinch, overhooks are also used to control your adversary. When utilizing overhooks, encompass both of your adversary's arms with your arms. In this position, control your adversary and utilize your lower extremity strikes.

Overhooks with Takedown

A Realistic Self-Defense "Crash Course"

Striking Combinations

The following are six striking combinations that will help you become accustomed to utilizing your striking techniques. In addition these combinations can be part of your predetermined self-defense gain plan. When practicing these combinations, remember that these carefully selected combinations, if practiced correctly, could help you to survive a life-threatening altercation.

Combination #1: Finger Poke, Hammer-fist

Combination #2: Finger Poke, Face Rake

Kuntao Jiu-Jitsu: Immediate Survival

Combination #3: Two Hammer-fists

Combination #4: Two Open Palms, Knee Strike

A Realistic Self-Defense "Crash Course"

Combination #5: Two Hammer-fists, Open Palm to Groin

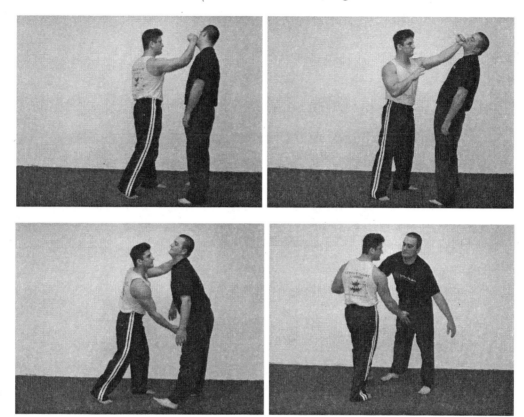

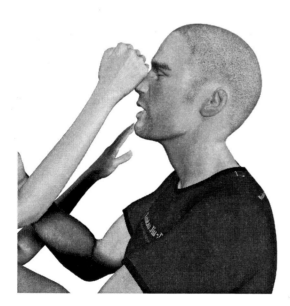

Vital Strike Review: Hammerfist

Use The Side Of Your Hand To Strike Your Adversary In A Downward Motion

Kuntao Jiu-Jitsu: Immediate Survival

Combination #6: Three Open Palm Strikes

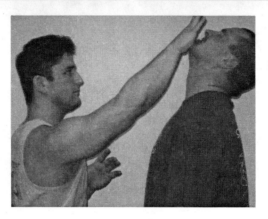

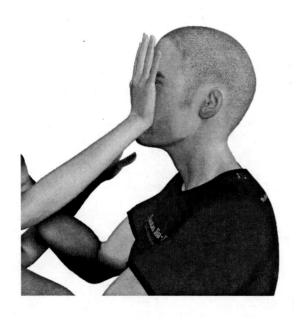

Vital Strike Review: Open Palm

Use The Palm Of Your Hand To Drive Your Adversary's Head Or Chin In A Backwards Direction

Chapter Thirteen: Defending Against a Striking Adversary

Keep in mind that defending against a striking adversary is harder than defending against one who places his/her hands on you. Why?

The Distance Factor

When an adversary is in close range, all vital areas (Chapter 8) are in reach. If you are close to your adversary's body more advanced joint locks, throws, chokes, and redirection techniques are all viable options (taught in the complete Kuntao Jiu-Jitsu Curriculum).

The major rule that you, and all Kuntao Jiu-Jitsu students must follow is that if you believe you are going to get into a life-threatening situation, strike first. Most altercations are "won," or the better term: "survived," by the person who lands the first strike. That is why we rely heavily on predetermined self-defense.

Now we understand that some martial artists may be offended by this revelation, but consider the following:

- Your life is just as valuable, or more valuable, than the adversary who has approached you.
- Your adversary might have incredible skills, such as boxing or wrestling that if he/she had the chance to employ would inhibit your chance of surviving.
- Your adversary might have a weapon.
- You do not know the intention of your adversary, but you do know yours: to get home safely.
- You can trust yourself that if you strike first and debilitate your adversary that you will not continue to inflict damage. Are you sure your adversary will offer you the same favor?
- Keep in mind that the paramount objective is to get away safely and back to your loved ones.

How To Survive a Striking Adversary:

Have a game plan ready (Chapter 7) and employ it before he/she can start theirs. Did you honestly think your adversary approached you without his/her own plan of attack?

Kuntao Jiu-Jitsu: Immediate Survival

If Punches Get Thrown At You First

Within this manual we will cover two strategies if punches are thrown at you first. The key to using each strategy is to go off your instinct. Instinctively, if you go to block the strike without any movement, try to use strategy one. If you instinctively backed up when your adversary tried to strike you, use strategy two.

Strategy One

When your adversary goes to strike you keep you hands up and move into the attack. Getting your adversary to move backwards is a vital key to your survival because when a person is moving backwards it is almost impossible to launch an offensive attack.

Strategy Two: Boxer

If your adversary is striking you and you either instinctively moved backwards or you cannot get in close, back up to create distance, solidify your stance (self-defense striking stance) and put your hands and arms extended outward. From this position lure your attacker close and use your leg strikes to the adversary's legs and groin.

Particle of Information

The complete curriculum teaches Kuntao Jiu-Jitsu students to stay in close to their attackers, clinch them to control movement, and then apply techniques or strikes from a clinched position.

A Realistic Self-Defense "Crash Course"

Predetermined Self-Defense

Your adversary confronts you in a threatening manner.

Step 1:
Use an open palm, as a pre-emptive strike, to strike your adversary in the face.

Step 2:
Grab your adversary's shoulders and send your right knee to the groin.

Kuntao Jiu-Jitsu: Immediate Survival

Step 3:
Clinch your adversary's head and knee your adversary in the face with your left knee.

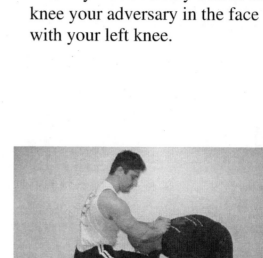

Step 4:
Repeat with your right knee.

Step 5:
Push your adversary to the ground.

Step 6:
Run to safety.

A Realistic Self-Defense "Crash Course"

Hook Defense Number One

In this scenario, an adversary approaches you and you instinctively try to verbally defuse the situation. Although you have followed the guidelines, (Chapter 9), you notice your adversary is becoming more enraged. When your adversary moves to strike you, step in close and start your defensive measure.

Step 1:
When your adversary approaches you in a threatening manner, assume your non-threatening position.

Step 2:
When you see your adversary attempt to strike you, step in, blocking the strike with your left hand while simultaneously using an open palm to strike the face.

Step 3:
Use your right front kick to strike your adversary in the groin.

Step 4:
Use your left elbow to strike your adversary in the face.

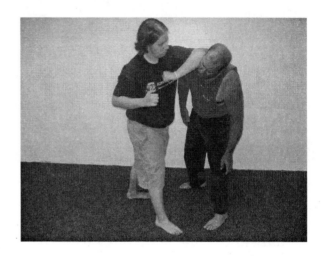

Step 5:
Use a right vertical elbow to strike your adversary's chin.

A Realistic Self-Defense "Crash Course"

Hook Defense Number Two

Step 1:
When your adversary approaches you in a threatening manner, assume your non-threatening position.

Step 2:
When your adversary goes to hook punch you, step on a 45 degree angle to the side and use both of your hands to block the strike.

Step 3:
Use your right hand to backfist your adversary's face.

Kuntao Jiu-Jitsu: Immediate Survival

Step 4:
Use your right leg to front ball kick your adversary's left leg.

Step 5:
Apply a Guillotine Choke (Chapter 14).

Guillotine Choke

Wrap Your Arm Around Your Adversary's Throat And Use Both Of Your Arms To Apply Pressure In An Upwards Direction

A Realistic Self-Defense "Crash Course"

Straight Punch Defense

Similar to the hook punch defenses, you first try to verbally defuse the situation, but your adversary goes to strike you with a straight punch. In this scenario, step on a 45 degree angle to the side. Simultaneously deflect the strike and use a closed fisted strike to hit your adversary's ribs.

Step 1:
When your adversary approaches you in a threatening manner, assume your non-threatening position.

Step 2:
When your adversary goes to strike you, step to the left and use your left hand to deflect the strike.

Step 3:
Simultaneously use a right closed fisted strike to strike your adversary's ribs.

Step 4:
Use your left oblique kick to strike the side of your adversary's right knee.

Step 5:
Follow through with your oblique kick and take your adversary to the ground.

A Realistic Self-Defense "Crash Course"

Step 6:
Encompass your adversary's neck with your right hand.

Step 7:
Grab onto your left bicep.

Step 8:
Finish by applying a rear naked choke.

Push Defense

In this scenario, your adversary is trying to physically intimidate you by pushing you around. Instead of allowing your adversary to continue, trap his/her hands and deliver a front ball kick to the attacker's leg. This well placed kick will start your defensive measures.

Step 1:
Your adversary confronts you in a threatening manner.

Step 2:
When your adversary goes to push you, trap his/her hands to your chest. Step back with your right leg to absorb the momentum.

Step 3:
Use your right frontball kick to strike your adversary's left leg.

A Realistic Self-Defense "Crash Course"

Step 4:
Grab onto your adversary's fingers and apply pressure downwards.

Step 5:
While controlling your adversary's fingers, knee your adversary in the face.

Step 6:
Continue the manipulation bringing your adversary to the ground. Control your adversary or break the fingers and run to safety.

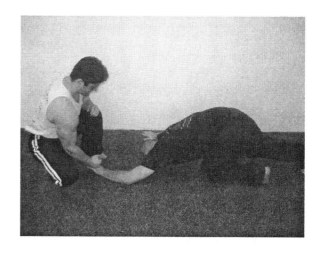

Boxer Defense

In this scenario, your adversary appears to have training in the art of boxing. When your adversary starts striking you with jabs and punch combinations, it is important that you are able to back up and extend your arms outward to create distance. This distance will prohibit your adversary from striking you with his/her hands. Use your leg striking techniques, including your front ball kick to break down your adversary. When your adversary leans forward from a well placed kick, move in and continue striking.

Step 1:
When your adversary starts to box with you, step back and extend your arms with the palms facing outward.

Step 2:
Use your leg striking skills, such as your front ball kick to strike your adversary.

Step 3:
When you stun your adversary use your right open palm to strike his/her face.

A Realistic Self-Defense "Crash Course"

Step 4:
Use your left open palm to strike your adversary's face.

Step 5:
Strike your adversary with your right hammer-fist.

Step 6:
Run to safety.

Kuntao Jiu-Jitsu: Immediate Survival

"Sucker Punch" Defense

In the "sucker punch" defense, you are trying to verbally defuse the situation when your adversary starts to walk away. Although it appears as though your verbal defusing skills worked, your adversary quickly throws a backhand towards your head. Since you never stopped looking at your adversary, you are able to block the strike and continue with your defensive measures.

Step 1:
When your adversary approaches you in a threatening manner, assume your non-threatening position.

Step 2:
You believe that you have verbally defused the situation and watch your adversary walk away.

A Realistic Self-Defense "Crash Course"

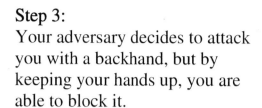

Step 3:
Your adversary decides to attack you with a backhand, but by keeping your hands up, you are able to block it.

Step 4:
Use your left open palm to strike your adversary's face.

Step 5:
Use your right ridge hand to control your adversary's head.

Step 6:
Apply a rear naked choke.
(Chapter 14)

Chapter Fourteen: Choking Techniques

In this section of the manual, we will go over choking techniques that will be used to help end a potentially violent situation. All choking techniques impede the oxygen supply to the brain. Although chokes are one of the most effective ways to end an altercation, if applied improperly or applied for too long, the choke can become deadly. When practicing with a partner, remember to follow the steps slowly, and make sure your partner knows to tap when he/she feels the pressure around his/her neck. Remember in practice, tapping out signifies that the technique is effective and is the signal for you to release the hold.

Guillotine Choke

Step 1:
With your partner leaning forward, encompass his/her head with your right arm.

Step 2:
Use your left hand to grab onto your right arm.

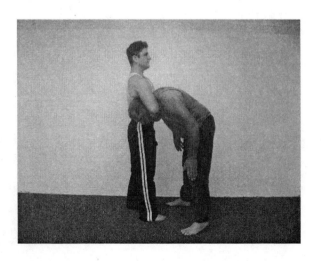

Step 3:
Squeeze your arms together and apply pressure upwards. When your partner feels the choke he/she should tap signifying to release the hold.

A Realistic Self-Defense "Crash Course"

Rear Naked Choke

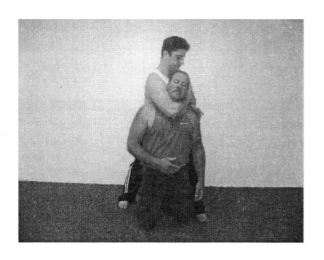

Step 1:
Encompass your adversary's neck with your right arm.

Step 2:
Place your left arm over your partner's shoulder and grab onto your bicep with your right hand.

Step 3:
Place your left hand on top of your partners' head and squeeze your arms together. Make sure your head is pressured firmly against your left hand to make the choke most effective.

Chapter Fifteen: Choke and Grab Defenses

This chapter is designed to focus on common street grabs and chokes and how to realistically defend against them. In the case where someone is trying to choke you, it is imperative that you first address the choke. Only after you have successfully stopped an adversary from choking you, can you continue your defensive measures. Although you may become very proficient in defending against the following attacks, when you are faced with a situation in which you know you are going to get attacked, you should not wait until the adversary grabs you. Use your predetermined self-defense and get back to your loved ones.

※Particle of Information: Concept Reminder

Remember when someone grabs you, he/she is using either one or both of his/her hands to grab you. This renders the hand (or hands) useless for punching. Attack the attacker, not the attack.

A Realistic Self-Defense "Crash Course"

Front Choke Defense

In this scenario, the attacker is applying a front choke with both hands. If it is effectively applied for more than five seconds, it will cause you to become unconscious. To counter the front choke, control your adversary's wrists and pull off the adversary's hands from around your neck. At the same time, use your leg kicks (either a front kick/knee to the groin or a front-ball kick to the knee) to strike your adversary. Effective striking will cause your adversary to lean forward. With your adversary leaning forward, use your Muay Thai front clinch to control your adversary and then utilize your knee strikes.

Your adversary attacks you with a two-handed front choke.

Step 1:
Immediately use your hands to come up and grab your adversary's wrists.

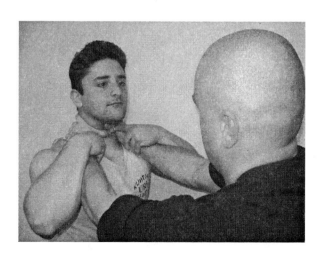

Step 2:
While controlling your adversary's wrists pull them down and outward at a 45-degree angle.

Step 3:
Notice how your hands are still above your adversary's hands.

Step 4:
Use your right foot to strike your adversary in the groin (front kick), shin (front-ball kick) or stomach (knee strike). This will cause your adversary's head to come down.

Step 5:
Clinch your adversary's head.

Step 6:
Use your knee to strike your adversary in the face.

A Realistic Self-Defense "Crash Course"

Step 7:
Throw your adversary to the ground.

Step 8:
Stomp your adversary's ankles, so he/she cannot chase after you.

Front Choke Variation:
In this variation, your adversary is running toward you as he/she applies a front choke. This scenario is similar to the previous defense with the difference being that you pluck off your adversary's hands while taking one step backward to stop your momentum.

⚛ Particle of Information: Front Choke
When applying a front choke, an attacker will always have his/her legs spread at some degree for balance. This makes your adversary vulnerable for a front kick to his/her groin.

Back Choke Defense

Many attackers will use the element of surprise to their advantage. Sneaking up from behind is a highly effective way to startle and often paralyze a victim with fear. To prevent this from happening to you, diligently practice all these techniques, and learn to react when you feel the initial touch. This section deals with two different defenses for the back choke. The first defense is similar to the front choke where you pull the hands off of your neck. The other defense is to throw your arm straight up in the air (reducing the surface area that your adversary can grab) and then immediately turn to face your adversary.

Your adversary attacks you with a back choke.

Step 1:
Immediately use your hands to come up and grab your adversary's wrists.

A Realistic Self-Defense "Crash Course"

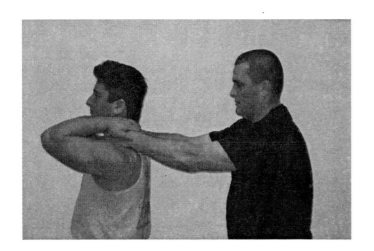

Step 1: Close Up
Notice how the defender is grabbing the attacker's wrist and thumb for control.

Step 2:
Pluck your adversary's hands downward as you move backwards into your attacker.

Step 3:
Shift to the right side of your adversary, while using your right hand to control your adversary's right wrist. Use your left elbow to strike your adversary in the stomach multiple times.

Kuntao Jiu-Jitsu: Immediate Survival

Step 4:
Turn in and face your attacker and use your right hand to hammer-fist your adversary's face.

Step 5:
Grab onto your adversary's shoulders and use your knee to strike your adversary's groin.

Step 6:
Run away to safety.

A Realistic Self-Defense "Crash Course"

Back Choke Defense Number Two

In this defensive variation of the back choke, you instinctively raise your hand, and turn into your adversary. If performed correctly, the choke will be released and you will be able to control your adversary.

Your adversary attacks you with a back choke.

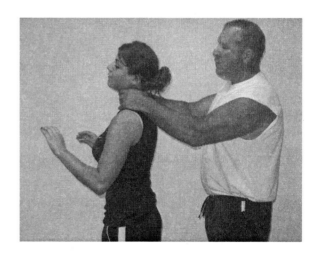

Step 1:
When you feel your adversary's attack, start moving you hands upward.

Step 2:
Shoot your right hand directly into the air, while you quickly rotate to the right side.

Step 3:
After you rotate you will be off to the side of your adversary, with your right hand control the wrist and with your left check the arm.

Step 4:
Use your right front ball kick to strike your adversary's knee on a 45 degree angle. This should take your adversary to the ground.

Step 5:
Stomp on your adversary's ankle.

A Realistic Self-Defense "Crash Course"

Side Choke Defense

In this scenario, your adversary attacks you from the side using a choke hold. To defend against this, immediately control his/her attacking hand that is on the front of your neck. Then use your closest arm to deliver several elbow strikes to your adversary's abdomen. Once you have stopped your adversary from choking you, continue with your defensive measures.

Your adversary attacks you with a side choke.

Step 1:
Use your right hand to pull down your adversary's choking hand, while simultaneously using your left elbow to strike your adversary's stomach.

69

Kuntao Jiu-Jitsu: Immediate Survival

Step 2:
Turn in and face your adversary and use your right hand to hammer-fist your adversary's face.

Step 3:
Grab onto your adversary and front kick the groin.

Step 4:
Throw your adversary to the ground.

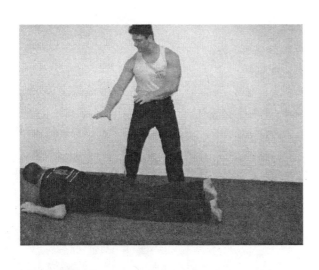

Step 5:
Stomp your adversary's ankles, so he/she cannot chase after you.

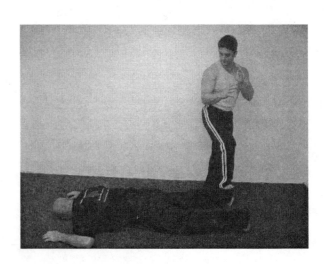

A Realistic Self-Defense "Crash Course"

Single Grab Defense

In this scenario, an attacker approaches you and without warning grabs your shirt (if there had been warning, you would strike first and run away). When this occurs immediately strike your attacker. If you can reach your attacker's face, hammer-fist your adversary's nose or use a finger poke to his/her throat. If the attacker is too tall, you can open palm or knee the adversary's groin. In this defense, we will assume that you can reach your attacker's face.

Your Adversary's Attack: Single Lapel Grab

Step 1:
Hammer-fist your attacker's face.

Step 2:
Hammer-fist your attacker's forearm.

Kuntao Jiu-Jitsu: Immediate Survival

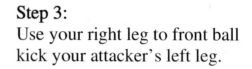

Step 3:
Use your right leg to front ball kick your attacker's left leg.

Step 4:
Clinch and knee your adversary in the face.

Step 5:
Throw your adversary to the ground.

Step 6:
Stomp your adversary's ankle so he/she cannot run after you.

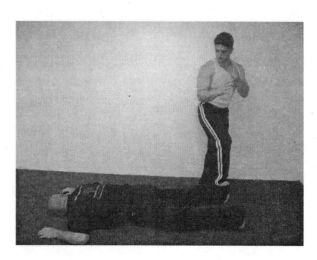

A Realistic Self-Defense "Crash Course"

Double Grab Defense

Similar to the previous scenario, the double grab defense is conducted when your adversary comes up to you and, without warning, grabs you with both hands. In this defense, we are going to assume your adversary pulls you in close. (If your adversary holds you at bay, use your leg kicks first.)

It is important to note that the adversary has given you a big advantage: he/she has rendered both hands useless by using them to grab you. If you react quickly and instinctively, your adversary will have no chance to continue his/her attack.

Your adversary attacks you with a double grab.

Step 1:
Hammer-fist your adversary's face.

Kuntao Jiu-Jitsu: Immediate Survival

Step 2:
Knee your adversary in the groin.

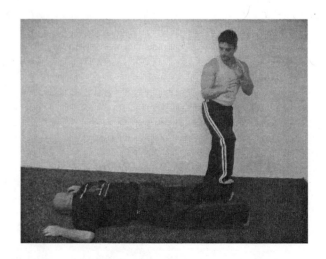

Step 3:
Clinch your adversary's head.

Step 4:
Throw your adversary down and stomp his/her ankle.

A Realistic Self-Defense "Crash Course"

Double Grab From Behind

When your adversary attacks you from behind, it is imperative that you turn and face your adversary as quickly as possible. With the double grab defense, you must quickly raise your hand in the air and turn in the direction of your attacker. When you turn in, be certain to control the adversary's arm and continue with your defensive measures.

Step 1:
When you feel your adversary grab you from behind, immediately raise your hands into your non-threatening position.

Step 2:
Raise your right hand straight into the air, and rotate your body toward your adversary.

Step 3:
Control your adversary by holding his/her wrist with your right hand and his/her shoulder with your left hand.

Step 4:
Use your right oblique kick to strike your adversary's leg.

Step 5:
Use your left hand to grab your adversary's face and rotate it backwards.

Step 6:
While controlling your adversary's face, use your left knee to strike the back of your adversary's leg (hamstring area).

A Realistic Self-Defense "Crash Course"

Step 6: Reverse Angle
From this angle notice the redirection of the adversary's head in conjunction with a knee strike to the back of the leg.

Step 7:
Follow through with the knee strike and take them to the ground.

Step 8:
Run to safety.

Pulling Wrist Grab Defense

In this scenario, an adversary comes up to you, grabs your wrist and pulls you in toward him/her. Contrary to popular belief, you do not want to pull away from your adversary. The correct defensive measure would be to go with the momentum and hammer-fist your adversary in the face. This will stun your adversary, allowing you time to finish your defense and get away to safety.

Your adversary attacks you with a pulling wrist grab.

Step 1:
Go with your adversary's pulling motion.

A Realistic Self-Defense "Crash Course"

Step 2:
Use your right hand to hammer-fist your adversary's face.

Step 3:
Use your right hand to strike the eyes of your adversary with a hard face rake.

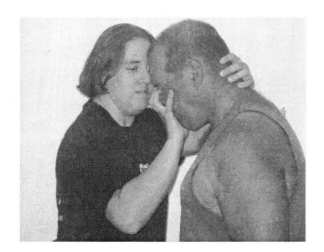

Step 3: Close Up
Notice how her left hand controls the back of the neck as the fingers of her right hand penetrate into her adversary's eyes.

Kuntao Jiu-Jitsu: Immediate Survival

Step 4:
Use your face rake to extend your adversary's neck backward.

Step 4: Close Up
Be certain to redirect your adversary's head backwards to offset his/her balance.

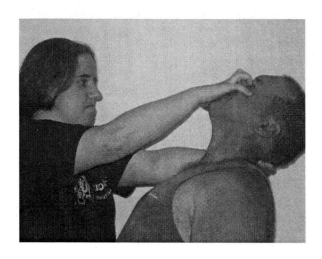

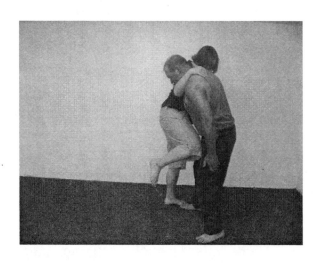

Step 5:
Use your right knee to strike your adversary in the groin.

Step 6:
Run to safety.

A Realistic Self-Defense "Crash Course"

Pulling Wrist Grab Defense Number Two

In this variation of the pulling wrist grab, we will assume that your adversary is too large to strike him/her in the face with a hammer-fist. Adapting the previous defense, when your adversary pulls you in towards him/her, we are going to use a closed-fisted strike to strike your adversary's groin. With your adversary leaning forward, continue with your defensive measures.

Step 1:
Go with your adversary's pulling motion.

Step 2:
Strike your adversary in the groin with a close fisted strike.

Step 3:
With your adversary leaning forward, knee your adversary in the head.

Step 4:
Use your right elbow to strike the back of your adversary's head.

Step 5:
Throw your adversary to the ground.

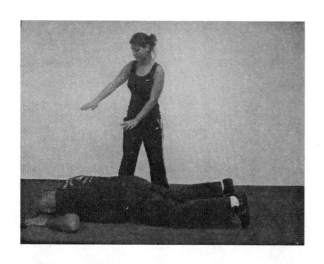

Step 6:
Stomp on your adversary's ankle and run to safety.

A Realistic Self-Defense "Crash Course"

Double Wrist Grab Defense

In this scenario, your adversary has grabbed both of your hands. Instead of using a complicated move to escape his/her grasp, attack your adversary's weakness. All of the attention is on controlling the movement of your hands, so use your low leg kicks to prime your attacker. Effective leg striking will free your hands and allow you to use them in your defensive measures.

Your adversary attacks you with a double wrist grab.

Step 1:
Use your right leg to front ball kick your adversary's left leg.

Kuntao Jiu-Jitsu: Immediate Survival

Step 2:
Turn your hands palm up and move your wrists in an outward manner, toward your attacker's thumbs.

Step 3:
While grabbing your adversary's face with your left hand, use your right elbow to strike your adversary's face.

Step 4:
If your adversary is still standing, use a lateral hammer fist to strike his/her face.

Step 4: Reverse Angle
Notice how the lateral hammer-fist is striking my adversary's nose.

A Realistic Self-Defense "Crash Course"

Headlock Defense Number One

If your adversary gets you in a headlock, your primary concern is to control his/her hand so the force (on your head and neck) is alleviated. This also prevents the headlock from becoming a choke hold. Due to the intense and dangerous situation of your adversary controlling your head, any rapid or sharp movements are not advised until your adversary's grip is broken.

Your adversary attacks you with a headlock.

Step 1:
Hold your adversary's arm (the one around your head) in close to your body.

Kuntao Jiu-Jitsu: Immediate Survival

Step 2:
With your other hand, ridge hand strike your adversary in the groin.

Step 3:
Pinch the femoral nerve inside your adversary's leg.

Step 4:
Drop down and put your shoulder into your adversary shin, applying pressure forwards.

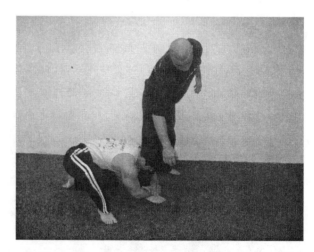

Step 4: Continued
Notice how the adversary is falling face first toward the ground.

A Realistic Self-Defense "Crash Course"

Step 5:
Take your adversary to the ground.

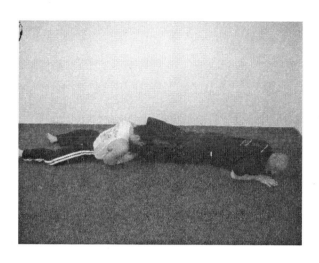

Step 6:
Get up and step on your adversary's ankle.

Kuntao Jiu-Jitsu: Immediate Survival

Headlock Defense Number Two

Your adversary attacks you with a headlock.

Step 1:
Use your right hand to strike your adversary in the groin with a ridge hand.

Step 2:
Pinch the inner thigh of your adversary.

A Realistic Self-Defense "Crash Course"

Step 3:
Drop to the floor and drive your shoulder into your adversary's ankle, while you hold the back of the ankle with your hands.

Step 4:
Take your adversary to the ground.

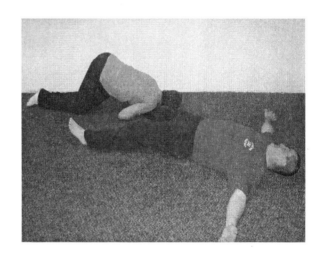

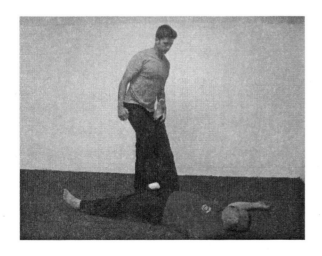

Step 5:
Kick your adversary in the groin.

Hair Pull Defense

An effective way to control a person is by pulling his/her hair. If an adversary uses this against you, you must first be able to turn and face your attacker. After this is accomplished, focus on breaking the hold using effective hand strikes.

Your adversary is attacking you with a hair pull.

Step 1:
Turn around and face your attacker and use your ridge hand to strike your adversary's groin.

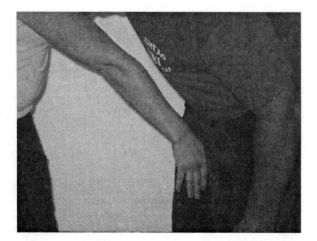

Step 1: Close Up
Use your ridge hand to strike into your adversary's groin.

A Realistic Self-Defense "Crash Course"

Step 2:
Use your right hand to open palm your adversary's chin.

Step 3:
Use your right knee to strike your adversary in the groin.

Step 4:
Deliver a knee strike to your adversary's face.

Step 5:
Throw your adversary to the ground.

Step 6:
Stomp your adversary's ankle and run to safety.

A Realistic Self-Defense "Crash Course"

Rear Grab Defense with Arm Grab

Using the element of surprise, your adversary comes up to you and grabs your arm while he/she covers your mouth so you cannot scream. When in this situation, make sure to first remove the attacker's hand from your mouth and scream as loud as possible. After that, continue with your defensive measures.

Your adversary attacks you from behind.

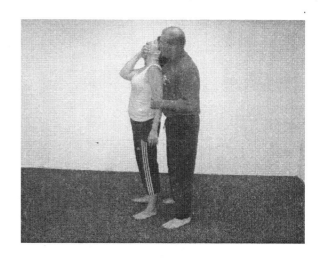

Step 1:
Use your right hand to remove your adversary's right hand from around the top of your mouth and scream loudly.

Step 2:
Turn into your adversary, whiling holding his/her hand to your chest. Do not allow your adversary to control your head.

Step 3:
Quickly turn into your adversary and use your right open palm to strike his/her groin.

Step 4:
Use your left hand to elbow your adversary's abdomen.

Step 5:
Use your left hand to hammer-fist your adversary's groin

A Realistic Self-Defense "Crash Course"

Step 6:
Use your right hand to open palm your adversary chin.

Step 7:
Apply a takedown using your rear heel strike.

Step 8:
Stomp on your adversary's ribs.

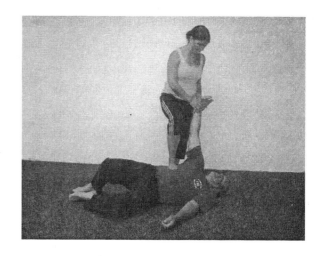

Front Bear Hug Defense Number One

A bear hug hold is when your adversary approaches you and grabs you around your waist – either with your hands pinned or free. As advised, you should never let anyone get close enough to apply a bear hug, but sometimes it is unavoidable. We will cover four bear hug defenses – three from the front, and one from behind.

Your adversary attacks you with a front bear hug.

Step 1:
Lower your center of gravity and place one foot back, so you can stop any momentum.

A Realistic Self-Defense "Crash Course"

Step 2:
Box your adversary's ears.

Step 3:
Place your thumbs into your adversary's eyes and move their head backwards.

Step 4:
Use your right knee to strike your adversary in the groin.

Step 5:
Using your front clinch, throw your adversary to the ground.

Step 6:
Stomp your adversary's ankle and run to safety.

A Realistic Self-Defense "Crash Course"

Front Bear Hug Defense Number Two

Your adversary attacks you with a front bear hug with your arms pinned.

Step 1:
Create space by placing your hands on your adversary's pelvis and stepping back with your right leg.

Step 2:
Use your right leg to front kick your adversary in the groin.

Kuntao Jiu-Jitsu: Immediate Survival

Step 3:
Use your right knee to strike your adversary in the face.

Step 4:
Apply a guillotine choke.

A Realistic Self-Defense "Crash Course"

Front Bear Hug Defense Number Three

In this front bear hug your arms are pinned. It is imperative that you create space so you are able to use your arms to defend yourself. Once you are able to create space, you can use your hands to strike your adversary's groin.

Your Adversary Attacks you with a front bear hug and pins your arms inside his.

Step 1:
Flex your knees while you lower you center of gravity. This will help to create space. Simultaneously, use your hands in a cupped fashion to strike your adversary in the groin.

Kuntao Jiu-Jitsu: Immediate Survival

Step 2:
Clinch your adversary's head.

Step 3:
Knee your adversary in the face with your right knee.

Step 4:
Knee your adversary in the face with your left knee.

A Realistic Self-Defense "Crash Course"

Step 5:
While controlling your adversary via his/her head, step to the side.

Step 6:
Throw your adversary to the ground.

Step 7:
Strike your adversary's head with the bottom of your foot.

Back Bear Hug Defense

In this scenario, your adversary is again using the element of surprise. Using his/her hands, the adversary comes up from behind and encircles your arms and waist. With the adversary being powerful, you must first hold his/her hands downward so the bear hug does not become a choke hold. If there is momentum involved, you must either go with it (perform a shoulder roll), or absorb it and take a few steps forward. If an altercation remains standing, use your backside (buttocks) to strike your adversary. If it goes to the ground elbow, scratch, pinch, and bite your adversary and get to your feet as soon as possible.

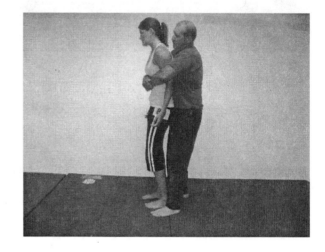

Your adversary attacks you with a back bear hug.

Step 1:
Use your hands to control the top of your attacker's hands. (This is performed so your adversary cannot move his/her hands toward your neck to apply a chokehold.)

A Realistic Self-Defense "Crash Course"

Step 3:
Use your buttocks to strike your attacker's abdomen or groin. Repeat this step until the hold is broken.

Step 4:
Face your adversary and use your right hand to hammer-fist your adversary's face.

Step 5:
Use your right front kick to strike your adversary in the groin.

Kuntao Jiu-Jitsu: Immediate Survival

Grab and Punch Defense

In this scenario, your adversary grabs your lapel with one hand and goes to strike you with the other. As with the single and double lapel grabs, the hand that is grabbing you is not an immediate threat. To successfully defend yourself you must first address the striking hand. After you have defended against the strike, continue with your defensive measures.

Your adversary grabs your lapel and tries to punch you in the face.

Step 1:
Use your right hand to block your adversary's striking hand.

A Realistic Self-Defense "Crash Course"

Step 2:
Use your right hand to open palm your adversary's face.

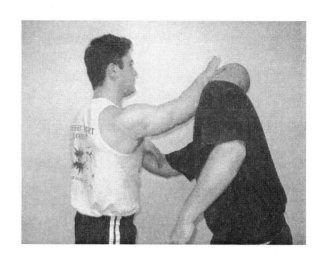

Step 3:
Use your right leg to front kick your adversary's groin.

Step 4:
Knee your adversary in the face.

Step 5:
Utilizing your front clinch, throw your adversary to the ground.

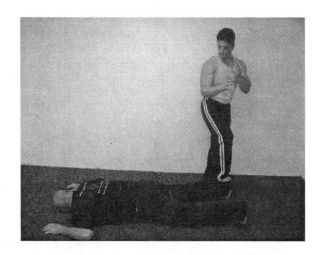

Step 6:
Stomp your adversary's ankle and run to safety.

A Realistic Self-Defense "Crash Course"

Automobile Defense

In the scenario where you are entering your car, there are a few safety tips you should keep in mind at all times. The first tip is to always look in the back seat of your car before you enter the vehicle. This is a crucial step that will help you to avoid a potential life-threatening situation with an adversary attacking you from behind. The second tip is to always lock your doors immediately after entering. Locking your doors will prevent an adversary from entering your car after you and attacking you inside. Finally, you should always park in a well lit area and have your keys in your hand at all times.

Your adversary tries to get inside your car as he/she pushes you to the passenger's side.

Step 1:
Use your right hand to peel your adversary's fingers off your mouth.

Kuntao Jiu-Jitsu: Immediate Survival

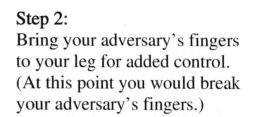

Step 2:
Bring your adversary's fingers to your leg for added control. (At this point you would break your adversary's fingers.)

Step 3:
Use your left hand to palm your adversary's head into your wheel as you punch him/her in the face. (Try to use your adversary's head to sound the horn.)

Step 4:
Thumb gouge your adversary's eye with your left hand as you open palm your adversary with your right hand.

Step 5:
Push your adversary out of your car and follow them to finish your defense.

A Realistic Self-Defense "Crash Course"

Step 6:
Strike your adversary in the groin with your right front kick.

Step 7:
Quickly re-enter into your car and lock your doors.

Step 8:
Drive to safety and call 911.

⚛ Particle of Information

Having a bumper sticker advertising your self-defense training can be a preventative step in avoiding an altercation. Remember, adversaries want an easy target, someone who will not fight back. Why would they take a chance with someone who advertises their participation in the martial arts?

Wall Defense Number One

In this scenario, your adversary pushes you against the wall as added leverage. The beneficial part of this scenario is that the momentum factor is taken out of the equation, allowing you to direct all of your energy into your adversary. When your adversary presses you up against the wall, perform a break fall as mentioned in Chapter 18.

Your adversary presses you up against a wall.

Step 1:
Use your right open palm to strike your adversary in the face.

A Realistic Self-Defense "Crash Course"

Step 2:
Use your right knee to strike your adversary in the groin.

Step 3:
Use your left hand to push your adversary's arm inwards, while you use your right arm to ridge hand your adversary in the side of the neck.

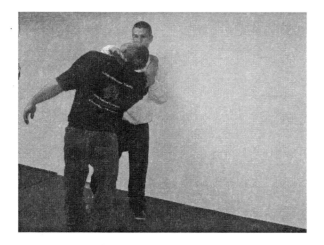

Step 4:
Rotate your adversary into the wall.

Step 5:
Use your right hand to hammer-fist your adversary's groin.

Wall Defense Number Two

In the second wall defense, it is imperative that you remove yourself from between your adversary and the wall. The key to accomplishing this defense is to turn your palm inward allowing you to roll off your shoulder and face your attacker. Doing this, will allow you to use the strength of your adversary in your favor, and allow you to continue with your defense.

Your adversary slams you into the wall from behind.

Step 1:
Turn your left hand so your palm faces your face. Then rotate in a clock wise manner, using your right hand to grab behind your adversary's head.

Step 2:
Place your adversary into the wall.

A Realistic Self-Defense "Crash Course"

Step 3:
Use your left oblique kick to strike behind your adversary's right knee, taking your adversary to the ground.

Step 4:
Box your adversary's ears.

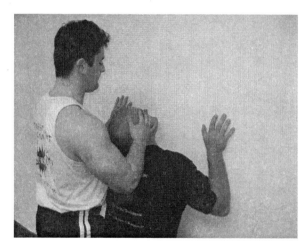

Step 5:
Slam your adversary's face into the wall.

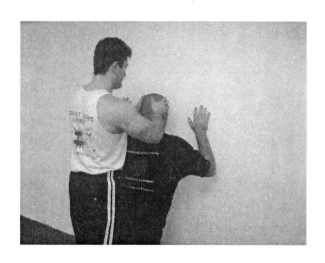

Step 6:
Stomp on your adversary's ankle and run to safety.

115

Chair Defense

When an adversary approaches you while you are sitting in a chair, you are at a great disadvantage. Due to your sitting position, the only defense that will be effective is your leg kicks to the groin or lower extremities of the body. After you have effectively used your leg strikes, you should immediately stand up and continue with your defensive measures.

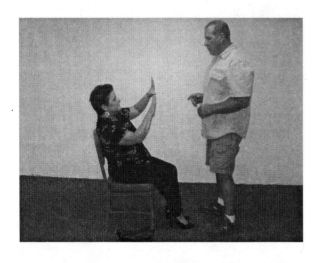

When your adversary approaches you, put your hands up in your non-threatening position.

Step 1:
Use your right front ball kick to strike your adversary's leg. Women should use their heels if applicable.

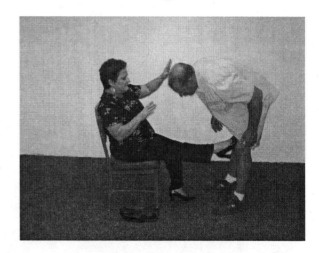

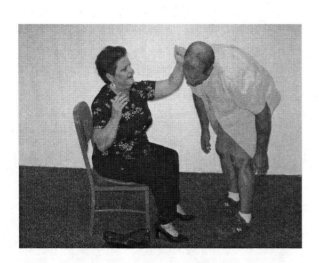

Step 2:
Strike your adversary with your left hammer-fist.

A Realistic Self-Defense "Crash Course"

Step 3:
Use your left hand and grab the back of your adversary's neck, while you use right hand to grab your pocket book.

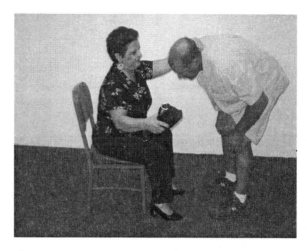

Step 4:
While holding your adversary use your pocket book to strike the side of your adversary's face. (You could also use a hammer-fist strike.)

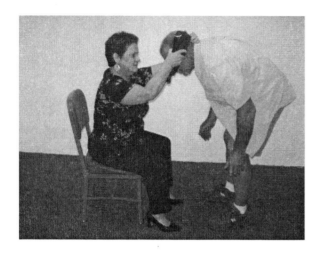

Step 5:
Stand up!

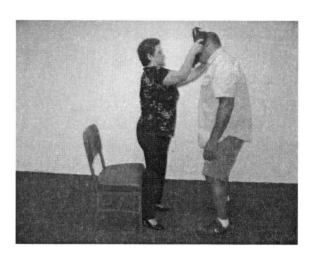

Step 6:
Front kick your adversary in the groin.

Kuntao Jiu-Jitsu: Immediate Survival

Chair Defense Number Two

You are sitting down when your adversary approaches you in a threatening manner.

Step 1:
When you see your adversary going to strike you, use your left hand to block and use your right hand to strike your adversary's groin.

Step 2:
Use your right arm in a circular motion to redirect your adversary off to your side.

A Realistic Self-Defense "Crash Course"

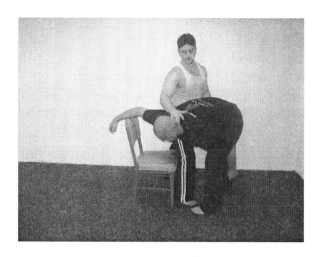

Step 3:
Stand up while controlling your adversary.

Step 4:
Rotate your adversary into the chair.

Step 5:
Notice how the momentum of your adversary's causes the chair to fall onto the ground.

Step 6:
Run to safety.

Table Defense

Similar to the chair defense, you are at a disadvantage when an adversary confronts you while sitting at a table. However, the table does put distance between you and your adversary making the adversary's attack more arduous. In this scenario, we assume that your adversary is trying to intimidate you by placing his hands on the table, while also verbally attacking you. If you feel you are going to be attacked, you must control your adversary's hands.

Your adversary notices you sitting at a table.

Step 1:
Your adversary approaches you and removes the items on the table, making a clear path from him to you.

Step 2:
He places both of his hands on the table to then verbally intimidate and attack you.

A Realistic Self-Defense "Crash Course"

Step 3:
Grab onto you adversary's wrists.

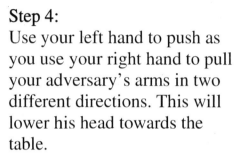

Step 4:
Use your left hand to push as you use your right hand to pull your adversary's arms in two different directions. This will lower his head towards the table.

Step 5:
Before your adversary can regain his stature, box his ears.

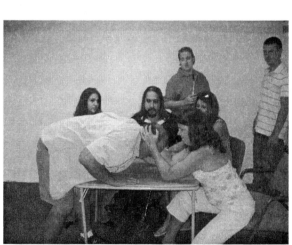

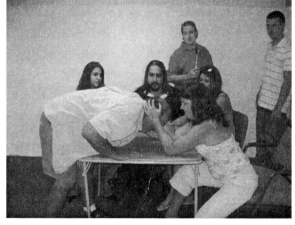

Step 6:
Force your adversary's head into the table.

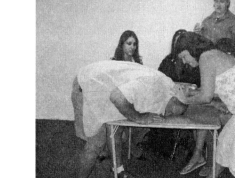

Kuntao Jiu-Jitsu: Immediate Survival

Optional Defense:
If there is a 3rd Degree Blackbelt sitting at your table, hold your adversary down, allowing him to pick up the pizza box.

Optional Defense:
Watch as he slams the adversary in the head with the pizza box.

If you believe the situation will only escalate, leave! In the case where your adversary chooses to leave the establishment, continue to enjoy your pizza.

A Realistic Self-Defense "Crash Course"

Defending A Peer

After collaborating with my peers and students, I decided to include a defense where an adversary attacks your friend, relative, or an innocent bystander. In addition to all the previous information, you must also understand how to remove an adversary from another person. In this defensive sequence notice how Eli secures the adversary, takes him away from the innocent bystander, brings him to the ground, and then runs to safety.

An adversary attacks a helpless bystander.

Step 1:
You notice the random act of violence.

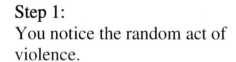

Step 2:
Move towards the aggressive adversary.

Kuntao Jiu-Jitsu: Immediate Survival

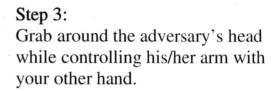

Step 3:
Grab around the adversary's head while controlling his/her arm with your other hand.

Step 4:
Pull the adversary off of the bystander.

Step 5:
Walk the adversary backwards to let the other person run to safety, while you increase your control.

Step 5: Close Up
Notice the position of the hands to control the adversary.

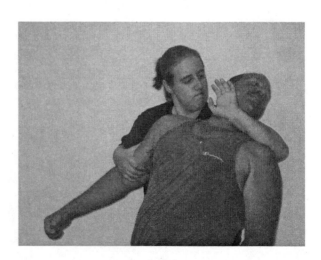

A Realistic Self-Defense "Crash Course"

Step 6:
Use your right oblique kick to strike the back of your adversary's knee.

Step 7:
Control your adversary as he/she falls to the ground.

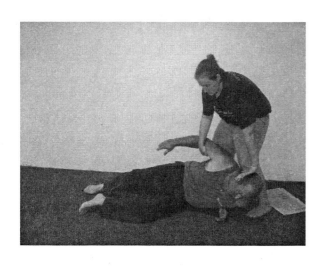

Step 8:
Push down on your adversary's head, to stop him/her from getting back to their feet.

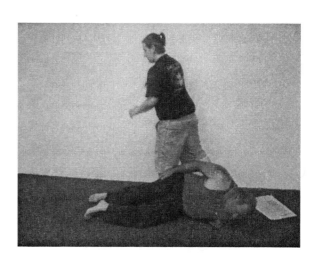

Step 9:
Run to safety.

Kuntao Jiu-Jitsu: Immediate Survival

Defending Yourself and A Loved One

One of the most terrifying situations is when you have to defend yourself, a friend, or a loved one, especially a young child. If at all possible you should try to flee the scene immediately, removing a child from harms way if need be. In a scenario where you cannot run away, move the person behind you and use your self-defense training.

Your adversary approaches you and a loved one.

Step 1:
Position your loved one away from the adversary, while keeping your hands up.

Step 2:
As your adversary continues for your loved one, use a front kick to strike your adversary in the groin.

A Realistic Self-Defense "Crash Course"

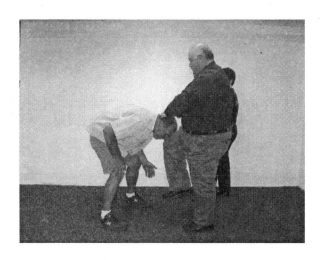

Step 3:
Grab your adversary's head and knee it with your right knee.

Step 4:
Use your left knee to strike your adversary's face, and drive your adversary backwards.

Step 5:
Place your hands on your adversary's head and shoulder.

Step 6:
Throw your adversary to the ground.

Step 7:
Stomp on your adversary's ankle.

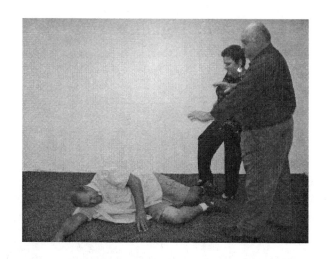

A Realistic Self-Defense "Crash Course"

Stick Defenses

In this stick defense it is important to note that the stick can be anything from a tire iron, lead pipe or a similar object swung at you with one hand. If at all possible, run away! In this and all scenarios in this manual, we are assuming running away is not an option. In the event that a stick is used against you, close the distance, and strike your adversary as soon as possible.

Your adversary swings a stick or similar object at your head.

Step 1:
Step in towards your adversary on a 45 degree angle and block the adversary's hand with both of your hands.

Step 2:
Use your right hand to backfist your adversary's face, while you grab your adversary's stick with your left hand.

Kuntao Jiu-Jitsu: Immediate Survival

Step 3: Close Up
Notice how the left hand controls the stick while the right elbow releases the adversary's hold.

Step 5:
If no further defense is needed, let your adversary run away.

Step 3:
With your left hand rotate the stick inwards (towards your adversary) and use your right elbow to strike your adversary's hand, disarming the stick.

Step 4:
Remove the stick from your adversary.

A Realistic Self-Defense "Crash Course"

Knife From Behind

In this scenario, your adversary attacks you armed with a knife. The key to this defense is to control the hand that is holding the knife. Throughout the entire defense hold that hand in a downwards motion, towards your chest. Since the muscular arrangement of the muscles that apply a downwards muscle, are stronger then those of your adversary's applying an upwards motion, you will be able to prevent the knife from touching your neck. As with all the techniques in this manual, make sure you practice this technique diligently. Please use caution and do not use a real knife when practicing this defense.

Step 1:
Use your right hand to hold your adversary's hand in a downward motion, into your chest. This will prevent him/her from moving the knife upwards to your neck.

Step 2:
Turn into your adversary while continuing to hold the adversary's hand with the knife.

Step 3:
Free your left hand by moving your hand away from your adversary's thumb. (Move towards the space between the thumb and index finger.)

Kuntao Jiu-Jitsu: Immediate Survival

Step 4:
Repeatedly strike your adversary in the stomach using your elbow.

Step 5:
Use your right hand to hammer-fist your adversary's groin.

Step 6:
Use your right elbow to strike your adversary in the throat.

A Realistic Self-Defense "Crash Course"

Step 7:
Turn into your adversary and open palm his/her face with your right hand.

Step 8:
Knee your adversary in the groin.

Step 9:
Pick up the knife and run to safety.

Modified Kuntao Jiu-Jitsu Defenses

In the event that you are unable to use your legs to defend your self, Kuntao Jiu-Jitsu can be very adaptable. Sensei Brian Baccaire trains under Soke-Dai Bochner and together they have adapted defenses to overcome his disability of Spina Bifida. In these defenses, notice how Sensei Baccaire is able to close the distance, keep his adversary close, and successfully defend himself. Although not shown in this manual, Sensei Baccaire would rely heavily on joint manipulations to subdue a much larger adversary.

Modified Hook Defense

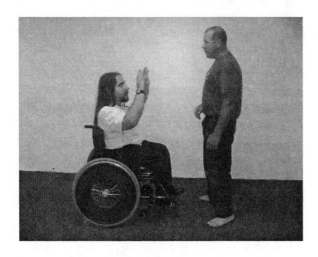

Step 1:
When your adversary approaches you, assume your non-threatening position.

Step 2:
Use both hands to block your adversary's strike.

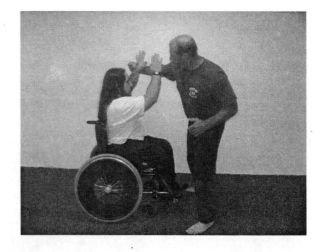

A Realistic Self-Defense "Crash Course"

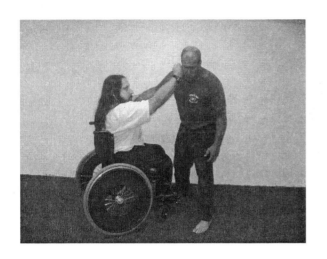

Step 3:
While controlling your adversary's wrist, use your right backfist to strike your adversary's face.

Step 4:
Use your right hand to strike your adversary's groin.

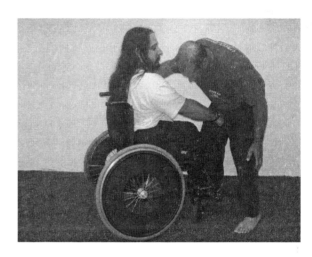

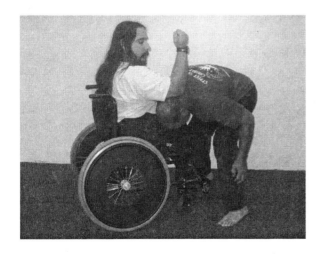

Step 5:
Elbow the back of you adversary head. Use Caution.

Modified Grab Defense

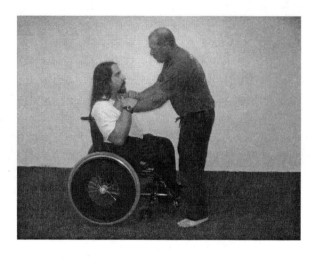

Step 1:
When your adversary grabs you, trap your adversary's hands onto your body.

Step 2:
Finger poke your adversary in the throat.

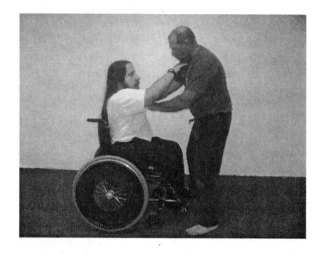

Step 2: Close Up
Finger Poke.

A Realistic Self-Defense "Crash Course"

Step 3:
Apply a finger submission.

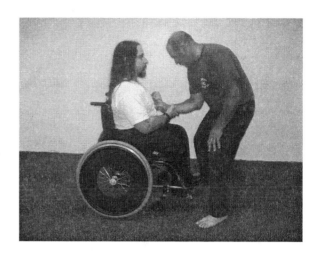

Step 3: Close Up
Finger Manipulation.

Step 4:
Bring your adversary downwards and apply a guillotine choke.

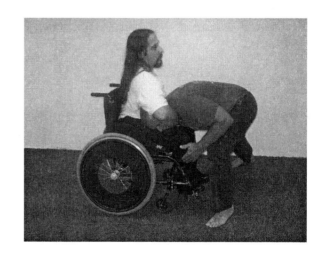

Chapter Sixteen: Rape Prevention

A successful martial arts style and school will always be able to provide women and men with quick and effective self-defense moves. This chapter deals with rape prevention in which the adversary has taken you to the ground and you are having difficulty escaping. These moves are taught at Kuntao Jiu-Jitsu rape prevention seminars and the self-defense crash courses. Additionally, these moves are also taught in the ground fighting aspect of the curriculum.

※Particle of Information: Fight Back

Most attackers are looking for the easiest prey. Immediately fighting back has proven to be a HIGHLY effective means of survival. Serial killers, such as Albert De Salvo, (Boston Strangler) have stated that when a woman fought back, he would immediately run away for fear of being caught. Do not be the easy victim. In fact, do not be the victim at all, hammer-fist them in the face!

A Realistic Self-Defense "Crash Course"

Rape Prevention: Defense Number One

Adversary's Attack: Mounted Position Your Hands Are Free

Step 1:
Strike your adversary in the groin with your closed fisted left hand.

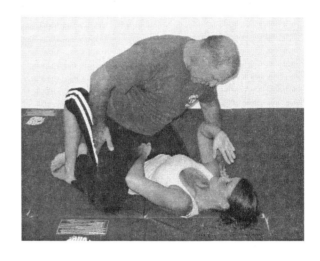

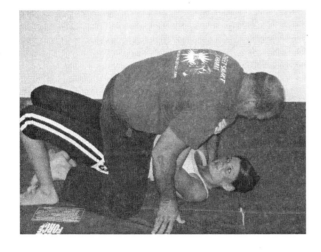

Step 2:
Use both hands to grab onto your adversary's chest. Extend your arms outward, while forcefully lifting your hips off of the floor, sending your adversary to one side.

Step 3:
Continue the motion while you roll on top of your adversary.

Step 4:
Use a closed fisted strike to strike your adversary in the groin.

Step 5:
Quickly stand up and stomp your adversary's groin.

A Realistic Self-Defense "Crash Course"

Rape Prevention: Defense Number Two

Adversary's Attack: Mounted Position Your Hands Are Pinned

Your adversary is on top of you and has your hands pinned.

Step 1:
When the adversary goes to strike or disrobe you, use your corresponding hand to post to the adversary's shoulder.

Step 2:
As you post your hand, use your hips to lift your adversary off of the ground.

Kuntao Jiu-Jitsu: Immediate Survival

Step 3:
Use your momentum to roll on top of your adversary.

Step 4:
Use your hammer-fist to strike the adversary's groin.

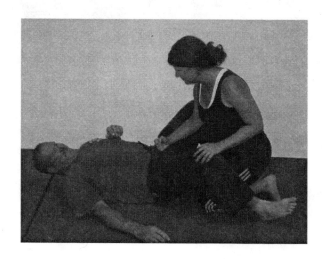

Step 5:
Use your hands to clear your adversary's legs and then knee your adversary in the groin.

A Realistic Self-Defense "Crash Course"

Rape Prevention: Defense Number Three

Adversary's Attack: Back Mounted Position Your Hands Are Pinned

Your adversary has you in a back mount with your hands pinned.

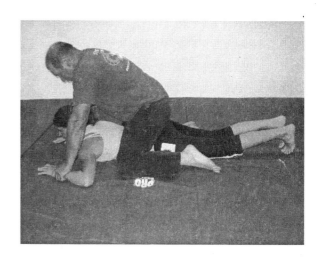

Step 1:
Move your hands together.

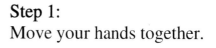

Step 2:
Use your right hand to grab your attacker's left hand.

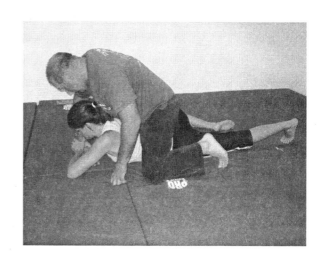

Step 3:
Throw your right shoulder into your attacker's right arm, positioning your right shoulder into your attacker's right elbow.

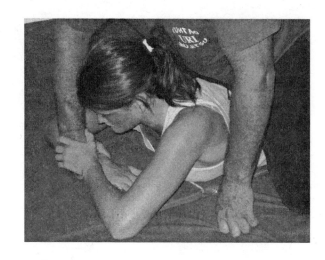

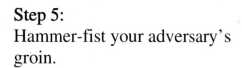

Step 4:
Use your body to spring forward and send your attacker forward. Work your way out from underneath your attacker.

Step 5:
Hammer-fist your adversary's groin.

A Realistic Self-Defense "Crash Course"

Chapter Seventeen: Using Your Keys

Using your car or house keys as a weapon can be an effective method of self-defense. To properly defend yourself, use your keys to strike vulnerable areas on your adversary's body. If you are planning on using your keys to defend yourself, they must be in your hands before your adversary approaches you. Getting in the habit of holding your keys in your hand when you walk to and from your car or house could save your life.

※Particle of Information: How Criminals Pick Their Victims

Most attackers will attack the easiest prey. Since this is his/her way of life, criminals have a keen sense for who the easiest victim would be. If you are holding your keys in your hand, there is a good chance that the adversary will think twice before attacking you. Holding your keys in your hand is one effective way to possibly stop an altercation before it happens.

How to Hold Your Keys:
1. Hold your keys in your dominant hand.
2. Extend your index finger so it can guide your key.
3. Use your corresponding thumb and place it on the top of your key. This will allow you to effectively direct the key into you adversary's vulnerable regions.
4. Clench your hand tightly.

Kuntao Jiu-Jitsu: Immediate Survival

Striking With Your Keys:
When using your keys to defend yourself you have a few striking options.

Option Number One: Stabbing
Take your key and jab it into your adversary's vital areas such as his/her eyes, throat, or groin.

  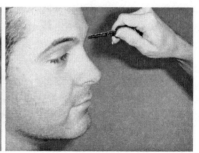

Option Number Two: Make an "X"
Take your keys and make an X on his/her face. This will startle your adversary and create an opening for you to flee the area.

Option Number Three: Combination
You can also combine option one and option two in addition to hand strikes and leg strikes.

⚛ Particle of Information: Using a Weapon
Keep in mind as with any weapon, if you use it incorrectly, it could possibly be turned and used against you. If you lose the keys, you must resort to your unarmed Kuntao Jiu-Jitsu Immediate Survival Training.

A Realistic Self-Defense "Crash Course"

Bonus Material

The following two chapters were included to enhance your chances of survival and over all safety. Chapter 18 includes what to do if you fall to the ground whether in the presence of an adversary or just around the house, Chapter 19, is additional information on how to control an adversary if you are fighting on the ground. In this chapter you will cover basic ground fighting positions and some joint manipulations to subdue an attacker.

Ground Survival *Ukemi*

Jiu-Jitsu Joint Manipulations

Chapter Eighteen: If You Get Pushed To The Ground

One thing that is certain in your life is that at some point, you are going to lose your balance, trip and fall. The art of Ukemi, one of the most critical parts of any martial art, teaches the student the proper way to roll and fall without sustaining injury. Learning how to defend yourself from different attacks without the knowledge of Ukemi can become a major Achilles' heal in your training. Since the art of Ukemi is beneficial while practicing Judo, it is important that it precedes any throwing or grappling technique.

Particle of Information: Ukemi Objective

The main objective of correct rolling and falling techniques is to protect your head and lower back. If either of these vital areas are affected, you will most likely not be able to effectively defend yourself.

Ukemi: Front Break Fall

The front break fall is utilized when the student is falling forward. Instead of using the wrists to break the fall, students learn to use their forearms to withstand the impact. When hitting the ground, your feet should be shoulder width apart, while you keep your backside up in the air. The front fall is designed to protect the practitioner's head, throat, groin, and stomach from striking the ground. At the conclusion of the fall, make sure you turn your head to the side, to protect your eyes, nose, and mouth. Remember to let out a loud yell or ki-ai, to control your exhalation rather then to have it forcefully expelled from your lungs.

How to Execute a Front Break fall:

Step 1:
Kneel down on a padded surface (mat).

Step 2:
While on your knees, fall to the mat using your forearms and hands to withstand the impact of the fall. Keep your elbows close to one another in order to increase the distance between your head and the floor.

Step 3:
Extend your legs outward. (This step is to be performed simultaneously with step 2.) Turn your head to the side and keep your backside up in the air, to avoid hitting your groin. Ki-ai, or let out a loud yell, to expel the air and tighten your stomach.

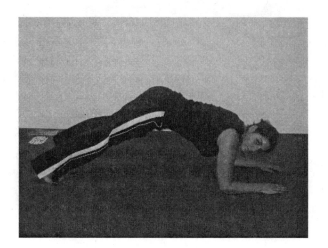

Turn Your Head To The Side and Use Your Forearms To Withstand The Impact

Keep Your Stomach and Groin Away From The Ground

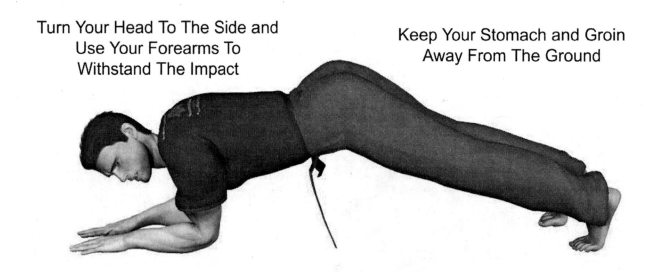

Ukemi: Back Break Fall

The back break fall is considered to be one of the more difficult falls to master. The main reason for this difficulty is the student's fear of falling backward. Beginning students should be instructed to sit on the mat and practice the steps below. When the student has a firm understanding of the back break fall, they can squat over the mat, and then eventually stand over it. When hitting the mat, tuck your chin to your chest and take the majority of the impact on your upper back. The back break fall is designed to protect the practitioner's head, coccyx bone, and lower back.

How to Execute a Back Break fall:

Step 1:
Sit down on a mat with your arms by your side. Tuck your chin to your chest.

Step 2:
Slowly fall backwards, striking the mat with the upper portion of your back. Keep your chin tucked to your chest.

Step 3:
Position your body so your lower back and buttocks are not touching the ground. Slap the mat with your hands (palms downward) and forearms to withstand the impact. Let out a loud yell, or Ki-ai and keep your chin tucked to your chest.

Bridge Your Pelvis and Hips To Keep Your Lower Back Off The Floor

Slap With Your Hands To Minimize The Impact

Keep Your Chin Tucked To Your Chest

Keep Both Feet Planted

A Realistic Self-Defense "Crash Course"

Ukemi: Side Break Fall

The side break fall is the most common fall from the judo throws. It is also utilized when falling from joint locks such as Kote-Gaeshi. Knowing the side break fall is very important in maintaining your safety in a dojo and/or street environment. The side break fall is designed to protect the practitioner's head, ribs, and lower back.

How to Execute a Side Break fall:

Step 1:
Start by standing on a mat and swing one foot in front of the other.

Step 2:
Slowly fall to the side corresponding with the foot you moved.

Step 3:
At the point of contact, strike the mat with your forearm and hand to withstand the impact.
Use your top hand to protect your rib cage, simultaneously use your top leg to crossover your body to protect your groin.
Ki-ai.

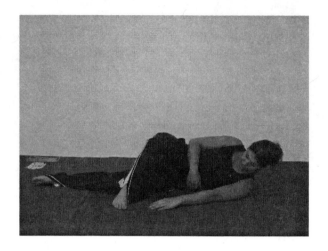

Withstand The Impact By Falling On Your Side. Use Your Arm To Protect Your Ribs and Your Leg To Protect Your Groin.

A Realistic Self-Defense "Crash Course"

Ukemi: Shoulder Rolls

The learning of shoulder rolls completes the Ukemi part of the curriculum. Shoulder rolls can be used as an alternative to break falls and in some cases can also be an offensive maneuver. In a scenario where you are attacked from behind, you can either choose to perform a front break fall or fall into a shoulder roll. An important advantage of rolling is that it allows you to get back to your feet quicker than a fall.

Beginning of a Right Shoulder Roll:
1. Put your hands in a non-threatening position.
2. Place your right foot forward and keep it pointed straight.
3. Your right arm firmly arches to form your support.
4. Turn your head to the left.

Middle of a Right Shoulder Roll:

1. Push off the floor from your left leg and fall into the roll. Your roll will start at the base of your pinky finger and continue from your right arm across your shoulder and finally finishing on your upper back.

Ending of a Right Shoulder Roll: End In A Side Fall

1. Land on your body on your left side.
2. Slap the mat with your left hand and forearm upon contact.
3. Your right arm is raised close to your body to protect your ribs.
4. Your chin is tucked into your chest to keep your head from hitting the ground.
5. Your left leg is extended outward while your right foot has crossed over your left leg. This movement protects the groin area.

Chapter Nineteen: Be Offensive On The Ground

In recent history, the martial arts community has witnessed the segregation of Jiu Jitsu into two main categories: self-defense and sport Jiu Jitsu. The art of Kuntao Jiu-Jitsu primarily deals with Jiu Jitsu as it pertains to self-defense. When the grappling aspect of Kuntao Jiu-Jitsu is taught, it is designed to address street fighting situations where eye gouging, biting, small joint manipulations, and groin strikes are all viable options. Students should utilize this training in situations in where they have fallen or been taken to the ground. Please be advised that grappling on the street will leave you unable to defend against multiple adversaries.

Differences between Street and Sport Grappling:

Street Grappling:
- There are no rules.
- It occurs unexpectedly.
- Multiple attacker situations can occur in a "street fight."
- Your adversary might be concealing a weapon, such as a knife.

Sport Grappling:
- There are rules. (No eye gouging, no striking to the groin, no small joint manipulations.)
- You can prepare for your adversary.
- There is only one attacker.
- There is a referee to stop the fight if you or your adversary cannot defend themselves.
- There are no weapons.
- There are rounds and time limits.

Particle of Information: Grappling

Grappling is most effective when defending against one adversary and is rarely ever effective against multiple attackers. However, in certain situations it may be more beneficial to take your adversary to the ground such as when fighting an adversary with good knowledge of striking skills.

Grappling Positions: Mount

The mount is considered to be the most favorable position in grappling. In this position, you are kneeling on top of your adversary with your knees on the ground. In the mount, control your adversary by using your striking and joint locking techniques.

Street Survival Option One: Strike your adversary in the eyes using a finger poke.

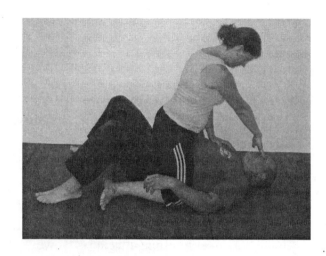

Street Survival Option Two: Box your adversary's ears while using your thumbs to strike the eyes.

A Realistic Self-Defense "Crash Course"

Grappling Positions: Side Mount

When you have the side mount on your adversary, you are lying across your his/her stomach, keeping your elbows and knees close to their body at all times. From this position you can control your adversary and use your Jiu Jitsu locking and striking techniques.

Street Survival Option One:
Strike your adversary in the groin with a closed fisted strike while using your forearm to apply pressure to the throat.

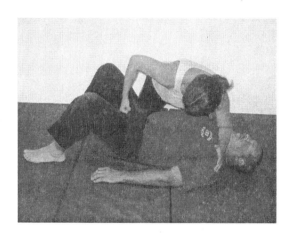

Street Survival Option Two:
Use your elbow to strike your adversary in the face.

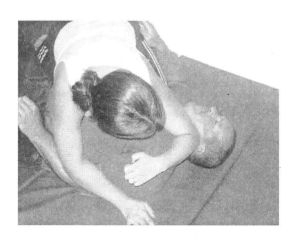

Street Survival Option Three:
Knee your adversary in the rib cage.

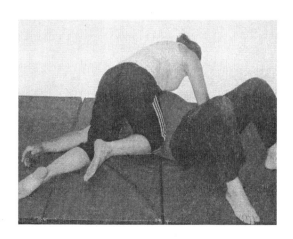

Grappling Positions: The Guard

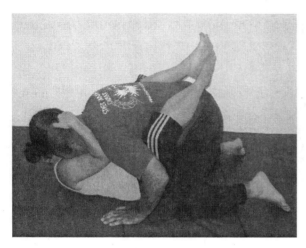

The guard is performed while you are on the ground lying flat on your back. In this position, wrap your legs around your adversary's waist and interlock your feet so your adversary cannot easily escape. Control the upper portion of your adversary by pulling his/her head into your chest. This will minimize the damage your attacker can inflict upon you.

Street Survival Option One:
Box your adversary's ears while using your thumbs to strike the eyes.

Street Survival Option Two:
Lift your adversary's head upwards and use a vertical elbow to strike his/her chin.

A Realistic Self-Defense "Crash Course"

Grappling Positions: Side Headlock Position

The side headlock position is when you are sitting on the side of your adversary while encompassing his/her head and arm. When performing this on the left side of your adversary, your left leg is bent forward and your right leg is extended backward. From this position, it is possible to control your adversary using chokes and armbars.

Street Survival Option One:
Strike your adversary in the face with a closed fisted strike.

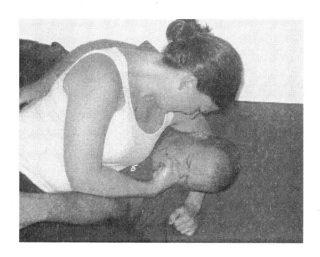

Street Survival Option Two:
Elbow your adversary in the groin.

Grappling Joint Locks

In this section we will cover how to control an attacker, or in a more severe case, damage a person's limb so they cannot continue to harm you. A joint lock is defined when you take an adversary's joint, such as a wrist, elbow, shoulder, knee, or finger, and bend it beyond its comfortable parameters. Taking a joint and manipulating it beyond its normal range of motion can be severely debilitating and cause a great amount of pain. This pain will assist you in creating doubt and confusion in your adversary, as well as changing his/her mindset from inflicting damage on you to avoiding the damage you are inflicting on them. This is why the main objective in physical self-defense is to strike your attacker as soon as possible.

Arm Bar From Mount

Step 1:
From a mounted position your adversary tries to grab or push you out of your mount.

Step 2:
Use your left hand to control your adversary's forearm, while your right hand controls your adversary's wrist.

A Realistic Self-Defense "Crash Course"

Step 3:
Shift your right knee to a flexed position and rotate your torso to the right.

Step 4:
While in a squatting position place your left leg across your adversary's face.

Step 5:
Hold your adversary's arm to your chest. Slowly roll back on the floor and move your hips upward.

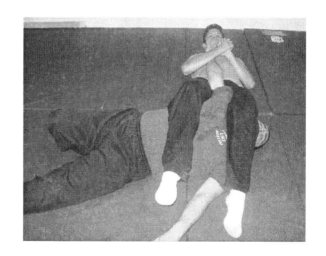

Upward Wrench From Side Mount

Step 1:
Start in a side mounted position.

Step 2:
Place your left elbow inward towards your adversary's face, and use your left hand to grab your adversary's wrist.

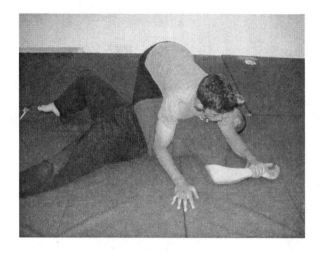

Step 3:
Your right arm snakes under your adversary's arm.

Step 4:
Grab your wrist and manipulate your adversary's arm upward.

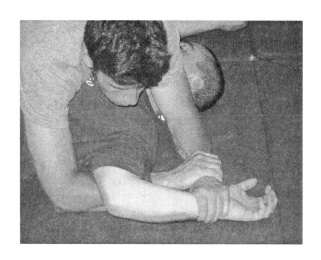

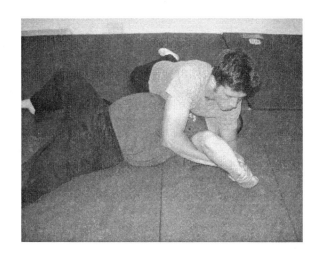

Step 5:
Rotate your position so your body is facing your adversary's knees. Continue to apply pressure until your adversary no longer wants to fight.

Kimura From Guard

Step 1:
Hold your adversary in your guard.

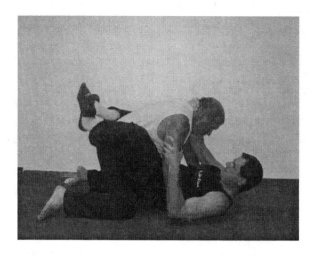

Step 2:
While maintaining head control use your left hand to gain control of your adversary's right wrist.

Step 3:
Using your right arm, come over the top of your adversary's right arm.

Step 4:
With your right hand, secure the Kimura by grabbing onto your left wrist. With the lock secured, position it inside your knee. Apply pressure upwards towards your adversary's head.

Chapter Twenty: Closing Comments

I would like to thank you for taking the time to purchase and read this manual on *Kuntao Jiu-Jitsu: Immediate Survival*. It is my hope that you have gained a new insight to realistic self-defense and what it entails.

I hope this manual has provided you with helpful tips and information that you believe will help you in a life-threatening situation.

Remember the key to effective self-defense is to keep it simple. Rely on your basic self-defense skills, intuition, and will to survive. Using all these attributes will make you capable of fending off any attacker.

If you would like more information about our system please visit our website at www.KuntaoJiuJitsu.com. On there you will find current Kuntao Jiu-Jitsu events, as well as additional books and videos on our system. Feel free to email us with questions, comments, or concerns.

Sincerely
Marc Bochner/Soke –Dai

About The Author

Soke-Dai Marc Bochner

Marc Bochner started his martial arts career at the age of eight under the tutelage of Professor Richard Petronelli in the system of Koba-Ryu. Under Professor Petronelli, Bochner learned the basic fundamental kicks, forms, punches and stances that are prevalent in all traditional karate based systems.

At the age of eleven, Bochner followed Petronelli to his Vee Arnis Jitsu School, where the focus shifted from traditional karate to a more effective and realistic form of self-defense, taught to Professor Petronelli by Professor Florendo Visitacion. After five years of dedicated training, Bochner earned a black belt in Jiu Jitsu under Petronelli and Sifu Albert Borino. At the age of thirteen, Bochner started to assist in teaching the children's classes. Three years later at the age of sixteen, Bochner started to assist in teaching the majority of the adult classes along side Shihan Bruce DiTraglia and Professor Petronelli.

On November 9, 1999, Bochner was the personal Uki (person who gets demonstrated upon) for Professor Petronelli when he successfully tested in front of the Head Founders and Head Family Board of Directors. In this examination, Professor Petronelli presented his reality based self-defense curriculum and thus validated his own system of Kuntao Jiu-Jitsu. As a result of this approval, Professor Petronelli was now known as the Soke (Creator of a System) of Kuntao Jiu-Jitsu. For all his years of dedicated training, Bochner was named Soke-Dai of the system (sole inheritor of Kuntao Jiu-Jitsu) and became the youngest person to ever hold that title.

In March of 2000, Soke-Dai Bochner was inducted into the World Martial Arts Hall of Fame for instructor of the year. In March of 2001, the Cranston Herald published a news article about Soke-Dai Bochner and the adaptive art of Kuntao Jiu-Jitsu. The article describes how Soke-Dai Bochner modified the system so that Brian Baccaire, a man with Spina Bifida, could still be able to effectively defend himself.

Kuntao Jiu-Jitsu: Immediate Survival

In the summer of 2001, Soke-Dai Bochner assisted the Rhode Island Justice Program as one of the local instructors who participated in the Kick Drugs Out Of Delinquency Program for the inner city children. In this program, Bochner and other martial artists demonstrated and explained the mentality behind martial arts to these youths.

Bochner is the designer of a 12-class "Nucleus" crash course that teaches instinctive reactions and defenses against common street attacks. Bochner is also the creator of the Kuntao Jiu-Jitsu children's curriculum which provides children and teenagers with the proper knowledge of how to realistically defend themselves and prevent possible abduction.

In March of 2004, Soke-Dai Bochner tested and passed his 5th degree black belt test. (An excerpt from this test can be found at www.KuntaoJiuJitsu.com.)

In May 2006, Soke-Dai Bochner received his Bachelors Degree in Exercise Science from the University of Rhode Island. He is currently continuing his studies, working toward his doctorate in Physical Therapy at the University of Rhode Island.

In March of 2007, Soke-Dai Bochner produced the official Kuntao Jiu-Jitsu Six DVD Training Set; *Kuntao Jiu-Jitsu: Your DVD Guide to Realistic Self-Defense and Street Survival*. These are the only DVDs showing the effective techniques within the art of Kuntao Jiu-Jitsu. In September of 2007, the 2nd edition of *Kuntao Jiu-Jitsu: Your Guide to Realistic Self-Defense and Street Survival* was published. In March of 2008, Soke-Dai Bochner plans to release his third book geared toward children entitled *Kuntao Jiu-Jitsu: Practical Self-Defense For Children and Teenagers*.

Currently, Soke-Dai Bochner holds self-defense and rape prevention seminars at the University of Rhode Island, Rhode Island College, Salve Regina University, and Bentley College. He is president and co-founder of the University of Rhode Island Kuntao Jiu-Jitsu club and is currently the head instructor at the Kuntao Jiu-Jitsu academy in Johnston, Rhode Island.

Soke-Dai with his father, Morris Bochner

A Realistic Self-Defense "Crash Course"

The more knowledge you possess, the more problems you can mend. In order to effectively apply your knowledge, you must train in a realistic, intense, yet controlled manner, which enhances your ability to survive.

- Soke-Dai Bochner

Founder of Kuntao Jiu-Jitsu

Soke Richard Petronelli has devoted over forty years of his life to the study of the martial arts. As a young child he was enrolled in his first martial arts class under Sensei John Lee in the art of Jiu Jitsu. Sensei Lee was a dedicated instructor who instilled valuable knowledge into the impressionable martial artist. He taught a young Petronelli not only the basic concepts of Jiu Jitsu, but also the importance of hard work and dedication. In 1962, five years after commencing his training in the martial arts, Soke Petronelli switched martial art disciplines to train under Master Peter Deblaiso in traditional Karate.

During Soke Petronelli's tutelage under Master Deblaiso, he was introduced to an instructor named Peter Rogers. After a brief conversation, Petronelli became intrigued by the hybrid style of martial arts that Master Peter Rogers taught. Embedded with a strong desire to expand his knowledge of the martial arts, Petronelli started training in the art of Koba-Ryu, an eclectic style that mixed Korean, Okinawan, Burmese, and American fighting systems. Throughout his fifteen years of dedicated training under Master Peter Rogers, Petronelli learned trust, discipline, respect, and harmony between life and the martial arts.

Continuing on in his quest for knowledge, Soke Petronelli initiated further training with former World's Strongest Man Professor John Wooten in the art of Miyama Ryu Combat Jiu Jitsu. Learning and formulating his own ideas and methods, Soke Petronelli continued training with Master Rogers, Professor Wooten, and Kung Fu instructors Master Shoon Yip, Master Charlie Hu, and Master Chong L. Woo. From 1957 through 1987, Soke Petronelli's martial arts knowledge included Combat Jiu Jitsu, Karate, Kung Fu, Wing Chun, and Judo.

In 1987, Professor John Wooten introduced Petronelli to the late Professor Florendo M. Visitacion, known to his students as "Professor Vee." After an initial and in-depth discussion of the martial arts, Professor Vee took the seasoned Petronelli under his wing. Drawing from his vast knowledge of Jiu Jitsu, Judo, Kuntao, Aikido, Gung Fu, and Filipino Stick and Knife fighting, Professor Vee showed Petronelli how he blended all of these systems into one effective fighting system, which he called Vee Arnis Jitsu.

While training directly under Professor Vee, Petronelli was given insight on how a true

A Realistic Self-Defense "Crash Course"

Grandmaster thinks and works. "Professor Vee taught me much more than how to punch or kick. I was taught about life – and how to give unselfishly these pearls of wisdom to my students. Martial arts is my way of life, and it is a devotion of love. Just like Professor Vee, I hope that the dedication and devotion that I show to the art of Kuntao Jiu-Jitsu will impact and inspire my students. I owe it to Professor Vee and my fellow instructors to expand on their teachings."

The thirteen-year relationship between Professor Vee and Professor Petronelli grew into a close bond that lasted until Professor Vee's passing on January 4th, 1999. Professor Petronelli made the three-hour drive to return to the Bronx, New York, where he had first learned the art of Vee Arnis Jitsu, to pay tribute to this great man. On November 5th, 1999, with the passing of his mentor still on his mind, the inspired Petronelli presented his newly created system of Kuntao Jiu-Jitsu in front of the same World Head Martial Arts Council that approved Professor Vee's Vee Arnis Jitsu. The overwhelming approval of Richard Petronelli's street orientated Jiu Jitsu style earned him the validation of his own system, Kuntao Jiu-Jitsu and the title of Soke (Founder of a martial art system).

Soke Petronelli's accomplishments in the martial arts include inductions into both the United Martial Arts Hall of Fame and the Vee-Arnis-Jitsu Hall of Fame. He is a member of the Head Family Board of the International Society of Head Founders, and is an elected executive officer of the Kokon Ryu Bujutsu Renmei Federation. Soke Petronelli has also been inducted into the World Martial Arts Hall of Fame and elected Executive Chairman of the board.

In addition to teaching selected black belts, Soke Petronelli conducts seminars across the United States, the U.S. Virgin Island and Japan, teaching alongside martial art masters such as Dan Inosanto (Bruce Lee's student), Paul Vunak (Jeet Kune Do), and Professor Wally Jay (Small Circle Jiu Jitsu).

Kuntao Jiu-Jitsu Instructors

Professor Bruce DiTraglia

At the age of nineteen, Professor Bruce DiTraglia began training in the martial art style of Kumiuchi Jiu-Jitsu. Professor DiTraglia trained for twelve years and achieved the rank of 1st Dan (Shodan). He continued local and private training with law enforcement agencies and various martial artists over the next ten years. This resulted in his mastering of many martial art styles including Jiu Jitsu, Kumiuchi Jiu-Jitsu, Combat Jiu-Jitsu, Judo, Aikido, Arnis, and weapon techniques.

In 1987, Professor DiTraglia was introduced to Soke Richard Petronelli and began studying Vee Arnis Jitsu under the direction of Professor Visitacion.

While teaching and continuing to study over the next fifteen years, Professor DiTraglia has achieved the rank of eighth degree black belt under Soke Petronelli. He also assisted in the development of the new hybrid art of Kuntao Jiu-Jitsu.

Professor DiTraglia's thirty-seven years of experience has taught him a vast degree of knowledge and character that he willingly shares with all of his students, including Soke-Dai Bochner, Sensei Brian Baccaire, and Sensei Matthew Mendillo.

Currently Professor DiTraglia is heading Kuntao Jiu-Jitsu's Weapon Survival Classes.

Professor DiTraglia with Kuntao Jiu-Jitsu Sensei Tessa Iannelli

A Realistic Self-Defense "Crash Course"

Dr. Matthew Mendillo, D.C.

Matthew Mendillo has been a student of the martial arts since he was eight years old. He has been studying Kuntao Jiu-Jitsu from Soke Richard Petronelli since its inception in 1999. Prior to that, Mendillo was a student of Aikido, Jeet Kune Do and Kali/Arnis.

At the Academy of Kuntao Jiu-Jitsu, he met Professor Bruce DiTraglia and Sifu Albert Borino, two men from whom Mendillo has received an immense amount of knowledge and discipline. Sensei Mendillo earned a black belt under Soke-Dai Bochner and is now currently an instructor in the Kuntao Jiu-Jitsu Children Self-Defense and Child Abduction Prevention Programs. He also regularly assists Soke-Dai Marc Bochner in teaching the adult classes and is Soke-Dai Bochner's personal uki (training partner) in any and all demonstrations and self-defense seminars. Sensei Mendillo has given several lectures on the human body's nervous and skeletal systems in the hope of explaining how knowledge of the human anatomy will allow for self-defense with maximum effect, yet using minimum effort. He has given these lectures at several locations throughout Rhode Island, Massachusetts, and Connecticut.

Sensei Mendillo also assists Soke-Dai Bochner with the specially designed "Nucleus" program. This program was developed with the intent to teach rape prevention techniques to women. In addition to these specialized classes, Sensei Mendillo has taught numerous seminars on rape prevention to college sororities and campuses across New England.

In 2000, Sensei Mendillo and Soke-Dai Bochner began teaching self-defense seminars on the campuses of The University of Rhode Island in Kingston, RI and Salve Regina University, located in Newport, RI. The two also conducted a Rape Prevention/Awareness seminar for People Organized for Women's Equality and Resilience (POWER) at URI in late 2000.

In 2001, Sensei Mendillo and Soke-Dai Bochner successfully lobbied to gain recognition for the University of Rhode Island Kuntao Jiu-Jitsu Club. The club allows students to receive a basic understanding of Kuntao Jiu-Jitsu while doing so in a relaxed, friendly atmosphere. Sensei Mendillo is also the founder of the University of Bridgeport Kuntao Jiu-Jitsu Club in Bridgeport, Connecticut.

Mendillo received his Doctor of Chiropractic degree from the University of Bridgeport College of Chiropractic in 2006. His Bachelor of Science in Biology was attained at the University of Rhode Island in 2002.

In August of 2007, Sensei Mendillo was promoted to third degree blackbelt in the art of Kuntao Jiu-Jitsu.

He currently lives in Rhode Island where he continues to study and teach Kuntao Jiu-Jitsu to all those who wish to learn.

A Realistic Self-Defense "Crash Course"

Sensei Brian Baccaire

Born with Spina Bifida and confined to a wheelchair, Sensei Baccaire had extensively investigated various martial art systems to see if any were adaptable and effective for his situation. In 1999, Brian Baccaire was introduced to Soke Petronelli and Soke-Dai Bochner. Baccaire immediately felt comfortable with the two gentlemen and discussed his interest in the martial arts.

Soke-Dai Bochner then worked with Baccaire extensively to develop an adaptive version of Kuntao Jiu-Jitsu. The result has proven to be an effective and realistic means of self-defense for Sensei Baccaire.

In addition to Sensei Baccaire's modifications, he was required to learn the complete system in order to assist non-disabled students with the standard techniques. Sensei Baccaire's martial art training began in 1999 and four years later in 2003, he was tested and he received his black belt in the art of Kuntao Jiu-Jitsu. As a Sensei, Baccaire teaches youth and adult classes in Kuntao Jiu-Jitsu. He also teaches a specialized "Nucleus" crash course designed for self-defense and rape prevention. Sensei Baccaire has a degree in psychology from Rhode Island College.

In July of 2007, Sensei Baccaire was promoted to third degree blackbelt in the art of Kuntao Jiu-Jitsu.

Soke-Dai Bochner with student Sensei Brian Baccaire

How To Contact Us

Main Academy:

The Academy of Kuntao Jiu-Jitsu is located in Johnston, Rhode Island. The academy hosts many different classes in the art of Kuntao Jiu-Jitsu and Realistic Self-Defense. If you are interested in training at the dojo or would like us to conduct a seminar at your school or place of business please call us at (401) 943-4100 or email Soke-Dai Bochner (Sokedai@KuntaoJiuJitsu.com). You can also visit our website at www.KuntaoJiuJitsu.com

A Realistic Self-Defense "Crash Course"

The Official Kuntao Jiu-Jitsu Instructional DVD Box Set
(5 Instructional DVDs and 1 Bonus DVD)

$129.95

Approximate Running Time 6.5 Hours

Order Today at www.KuntaoJiuJitsu.com

DVD 1: Concepts, Striking, Clinching, Striking Combinations, Vital Areas

Chapter One: Main Objective In Self-Defense
Chapter Two: Self-Defense vs. Fighting Altercations
Chapter Three: Two Categories of a Self-Defense Situation
Chapter Four: Stages of a Self-Defense Situation
Chapter Five: Ranges of a Self-Defense Situation
Chapter Six: Hand/Elbow Strikes
Chapter Seven: Leg/Knee Strikes
Chapter Eight: Clinching
Chapter Nine: Striking Combinations
Chapter Ten: Vital Areas of the Human Body

DVD 2: Stepping, Ukemi (Rolls/Falls), Judo Throws, Takedowns

Chapter One: Essential Stepping
    Non-Threatening Position
    V Stepping
    Triangle Stepping
    X Stepping
    Star Stepping
    Paqua Stepping

Kuntao Jiu-Jitsu: Immediate Survival

Chapter Two: Ukemi
    Front Break Fall
    Back Break Fall
    Side Break Fall
    Shoulder Rolls
Chapter Three: Judo Throws
    Major Hip Throw
    Major Shoulder Throw
    Major Inner Reap
    Major Outer Reap
Chapter Four: Takedowns
    Single Leg Takedown
    Front Shoulder Takedown
    Around The Back Takedown

DVD 3: Jiu-Jitsu Joint Manipulations, Chokes, Street Grappling, Rape Prevention

Chapter One: Jiu-Jitsu Joint Locks
    Kote-Gaeshi
    Kote-Mawashi
    Sankyo (Kote-Hineri)
    Ground Manipulations
Chapter Two: Choking Techniques
    Rear Naked Choke
    Guillotine
    Adaptation
    Carotid Choke
    Front Naked Choke
Chapter Three: Street Grappling (Positions and Locks)
    Mount
    Side Mount
    Guard
    Half Guard
    Judo Position (Side Headlock)
Chapter Four: Rape Prevention Techniques

A Realistic Self-Defense "Crash Course"

DVD 4: Set Techniques/Student Created Defenses

Chapter One: Te's
Chapter Two: Kick Drills
Chapter Three: Muggings
Chapter Four: Double Muggings
Chapter Five: Additional Punch Defenses
Chapter Six: Student Created Defenses (Grab Defenses)
    Front Choke
    Back Choke
    Side Choke
    Pulling Wrist Grab
    Double Wrist Grab
    Front Bear Hug
    Back Bear hug
    Headlock
    Single Lapel Grab
    Double Lapel Grab
    Grab and Punch
    Chair Defense
    Wall Defense
    Wall Defense #2
Chapter Seven: Grabbing Defenses Additional Endings

DVD 5: Strategies Against Trained Adversaries, Stick Defenses, Knife Defenses, Gun Defenses, Scenario Training

Chapter One: Defending Against an Untrained Adversary
Chapter Two: Defending Against a Street Fighter
Chapter Three: Defending Against a Boxer
Chapter Four: Defending Against a Wrestler/Grappler
Chapter Five: Defending Against a Kick Boxer
Chapter Six: Arnis Stick Fighting
    Holding the Arnis Stick
    Five Angles of Attack
    Arnis Flowing Drill
    Twelve Points of Attack
    Double Sinawalli
    Flowing Drill #3
    Flowing Drill #4
    Flowing Drill #5

Kuntao Jiu-Jitsu: Immediate Survival

        Combining Flowing Drills
Chapter Seven: Stick vs. Stick Disarms
Chapter Eight: Stick vs. Empty Hand Disarms
Chapter Nine: Knife Survival
        Flowing With the Knife
        Knife vs. Knife Defense
        Knife vs. Empty Hand Defenses
        Knife Scenario 1
        Knife Scenario 2
Chapter Ten: Gun Survival
        Redirecting the Gun
        Gun to forehead Defense#1
        Gun to forehead Defense#2
        Gun to stomach Defense
        Gun to back of the head defense
        Gun to the side of the head defense
Chapter Eleven: Verbal Defusing
Chapter Twelve: Club Scenarios
Chapter Thirteen: Elevator Scenarios
Chapter Fourteen: Street Scenarios

DVD 6: Bonus Footage

Chapter One: Soke-Dai Bochner Blackbelt Examination
Chapter Two: Blackships Festival Demonstration – Newport, Rhode Island
Chapter Three: Professor Bruce DiTraglia University of Rhode Island Seminar
Chapter Four: Bloopers

Kuntao Jiu-Jitsu Training Manuals

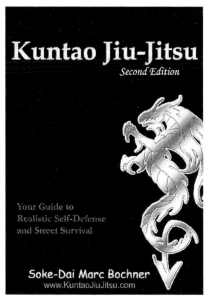

Kuntao Jiu-Jitsu: Your Guide to Realistic Self-Defense and Street Survival (2nd edition) is the official training manual of the Kuntao Jiu-Jitsu system. The manual is designed to give readers an insight into the concepts and techniques of the KJJ system. The official guide covers in depth self-defense concepts, Jiu-Jitsu joint locks, Judo throws and takedowns, ground survival techniques, as well as weapon defenses. This book is highly recommended for anyone interested in Kuntao Jiu-Jitsu or looking to expand their martial arts knowledge.

Retail Price is $24.95

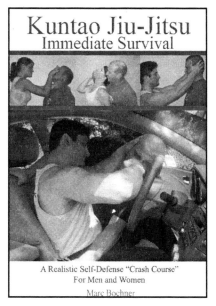

Kuntao Jiu-Jitsu: Immediate Survival serves as a "crash course" in self-defense for people who want to learn quick and effective self-defense techniques. A myriad of common street altercations are covered within this manual.

Retail Price is $19.95

Glossary

Aikido – a Japanese martial art that uses redirecting techniques to deter your adversary from continuing his/her attack

Arnis – the art of Filipino stick and knife fighting

Breaking the Punch – when you block your adversary's strike between the forearm and the bicep. (opposite side of your adversary's elbow)

Categories of Self-Defense – reactive and predetermined self-defense

Choke Hold – any hold that impairs the blood or oxygen to the brain

Clinch – a technique used to control the movement of your adversary

Concept – a general idea

Defusing – the skill of stopping a confrontation before it turns physical

Dojo – martial arts training hall

Escrima – see Arnis

Grappling – defending yourself while on the ground; similar to wrestling with the addition of joint manipulations and chokes

Ground Fighting – see grappling

Guard – a grappling position where you are on your back and your adversary is between your legs

Hybrid Style – a martial arts style that incorporates two or more pre-existing styles

Ippon Seionage – major one-handed shoulder throw

Joint Manipulation – bending a joint beyond its comfortable parameters, causing pain and compliance

Judo – an Olympic Sport that focuses on off balancing and throwing opponents

Jiu Jitsu – a Japanese martial arts used by the Samurai as their main form of unarmed combat

A Realistic Self-Defense "Crash Course"

Kali – see Arnis

Ki-ai – A loud yell that expels air from your body

Kote-Gaeshi – wrist turned outward

Kote-Hinerai – see Sankyo

Kote-Mawashi – wrist turned downward

Kung Fu – a Chinese fighting system that was based off the movements of animals

Kuntao – an Indonesian style of fighting incorporating elbow strikes, knees, and low lined kicks

Kuzushi – balance drills

Makiwara – body conditioning

Particle of Information – additional information that is conveniently located in throughout the book.

Mount – a grappling position in which you are kneeling over of your adversary

Muay Thai Kick Boxing – a style of fighting that originated in Thailand, which uses hand strikes, legs strikes, knees and elbows

O – Goshi – major hip throw

O-Soto-Gari – major outer drop

O-Uchi-Gari – major inner reap

Plucking – a technique that is performed off a chokehold that removes the attacker's hands from your throat

Predetermined Self-Defense – the type of self-defense in which you defend yourself by striking your adversary first

Priming – to initially stun your adversary using strikes

Ranges of a Self-Defense Situation – the variable distances that a fight can occur in

Reactive Self-Defense – the type of self-defense in which you defend yourself by reacting to your adversary's attack

Redirection Technique – a technique that rotates your adversary onto the ground

Sankyo – wrist turned inward

Sensei – martial arts instructor

Set Techniques – the core techniques of Kuntao Jiu-Jitsu in which students learn the basis of using all their skills in a unified manner

Side Mount – a grappling position in which your adversary is on his/her back and you are laying across keeping your elbows and knees close to his/her body

Soke – founder of a martial arts system

Soke – Dai – inheritor of a martial arts system; one who teaches in place of a Soke

Stages of a Self-Defense Situation – an outline of objectives to survive an altercation

Strangle Hold – see choke hold

Takedown – a technique in which you render your adversary to the ground

Tapping Out – a signal that indicates a move's effectiveness; when you tap out your partner will release the move

Te – hand

Techniques – basic physical movements

Throw – a technique in which your offset your adversary's balance and remove them from him/her feet

Ukemi – the art of rolling and falling

Uki – person who gets demonstrated upon

Yamai – a command indicating to stop what you are doing and focus on the main instructor

Reference List

De Becker, Gavin. 1997. *The Gift Of Fear.* New York, New York: Dell Publishing.

Hall, Susan J. 2003. *Basic Biomechanics, fourth edition.* Boston: The McGraw Hill Companies, Inc.

ISBN 1425151b5-5